The

PLEASURE OF GARDENING

ROCK &
ALPINE GARDENS

A complete practical guide

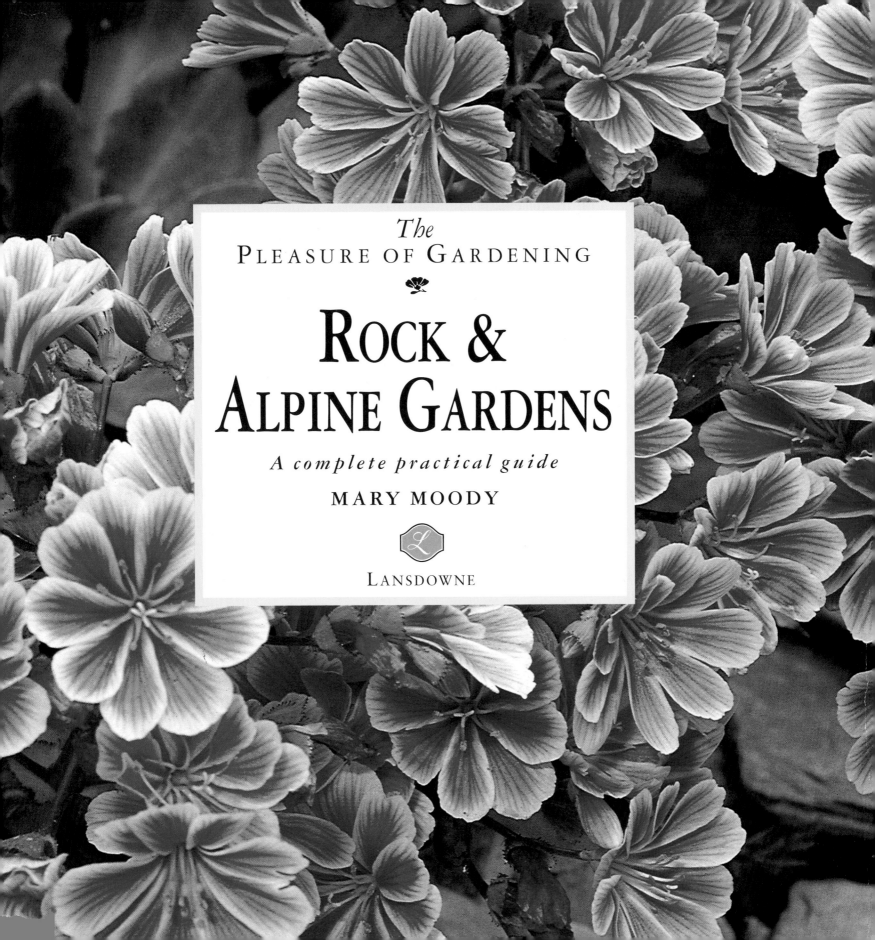

The
PLEASURE OF GARDENING

❀

ROCK & ALPINE GARDENS

A complete practical guide

MARY MOODY

L

LANSDOWNE

CONTENTS

INTRODUCTION 7

Introduction

There are many different aspects and styles of gardening to fascinate and delight the enthusiast, from orchid-growing to the cultivation of fragrant herbs and spices. Each area has its own band of dedicated followers. Rock gardening is one aspect that appeals to a wide range of people, from new gardeners to those who have been gardening all their lives.

Rock gardens are man-made environments that are used specifically for the cultivation of low-growing plants that thrive in the well-drained soil pockets between rocks. The types of plants that enjoy these conditions vary considerably, and include many varieties that are native to warm or temperate regions of the globe, as well as alpine plants that are found growing on rocky mountain slopes above the tree line.

For many devotees, growing alpines is the natural progression from growing annuals and perennials, although it is

LEFT: The time spent in establishing a rockery garden will determine its on-going success; it must be solidly built, well drained and completely weed-free to maintain thriving plants.

regarded as a more refined and more exacting science. The prospect of growing many of these delightful small plants need not be a daunting one, although it is true to say that a badly executed rock garden, or "rockery", can end up as a gardener's nightmare, overrun with weeds and unhappy plants that are struggling to compete for moisture and nutrients. While "true" alpine gardening is highly specialized and requires a good knowledge of the particular requirements of each individual plant, there are plenty of hardy and easy-to grow rockery plants that will bring tremendous satisfaction, and create a beautiful effect. If it is well planned and planted with care and thoughtfulness, such a garden can be one of nature's great joys, filled with fascinating, low-growing plants happily nestled and thriving in the pockets of soil between the rocks.

Rock garden enthusiasts take various approaches to the design of their garden. Most opt for a natural approach with the layout of rocks, because a more stylized arrangement looks artificial and therefore does not complement the beauty of the plants. Chapter Three describes how you can achieve the effect of a natural-looking garden.

The choice of species to be grown in the garden will depend greatly on the climate and the soil in the district where the garden is located. True alpine gardens can only be grown in climates where winters are cool to cold, but frosts and cold winds are not too severe. In many northern hemisphere gardens, alpine houses are constructed specifically for the cultivation of these plants, providing shelter in winter where necessary. In more temperate climates, a wider range of plants can be used in the rock garden. Here plants will be chosen for their growth habit (generally, low-growing, hummock-forming varieties are suitable for the rock garden), and their ability to thrive in the well-drained soil provided.

In this title in *The Pleasure of Gardening* series, I have aimed to simplify the process of planning and planting a rock garden. I have also detailed alternative ways of growing alpine plants, for those gardeners whose climate is not sympathetic to the more sensitive species that need winter protection from damp and wind. The intention of this book is to provide inspiration and encouragement: the keen gardener will find wonderful results are well within reach with a rock or alpine garden.

CREATING A ROCK OR ALPINE GARDEN

A Popular Style Evolves

Rock gardens and alpine gardens are well-established landscaping styles that are used in many countries around the world, with varying degrees of success.

Once you have decided to create this type of garden, how you succeed will depend on many factors, including the type of plants you choose and the environment in which they grow. While rock gardens, or "rockeries", were originally created specifically for the growing of alpine plants, this is no longer necessarily the case. Gardeners all over the world now have the freedom and the scope to cultivate a wide range of plants that enjoy the particular growing environment these gardens provide.

OPPOSITE: In its broad context a rockery garden can be used to provide a healthy growing environment for a wide range of plants including bulbs and ground-covers, as well as traditional alpine plants.

PREVIOUS PAGE: The exquisite white flowers of the wood anemone (Anemone nemorosa), which are flushed with palest pink, cover the plants in mid to late summer. Found growing in native woodland and mountain pastures.

The first alpine and rock gardens were cultivated in the late 1700s, with wild plants carried back to Great Britain by intrepid explorers and botanists who had just started venturing into the world's most mountainous regions. The first rockery designed specifically for growing alpines was in the Chelsea Physic Garden, in the year 1772. The style quickly became very popular, although many of the more sensitive plants failed to thrive away from their natural environment. As a result, a variety of planting techniques, such as scree beds, built-up rock gardens, and alpine houses, were developed to increase the success rate for growing the more vulnerable exotic species.

A rock garden can take many forms: it may be a small feature in one area of your garden, or it may even occupy your entire garden area. In Victorian times, rockeries first appeared as a focal feature in the garden, with the main emphasis being on the actual arrangement of the rocks. Over the years the style evolved, and in time plants were introduced to soften the impact of the mounds of rock, and to provide a display for all those newly discovered alpine varieties.

Like all styles of gardening, rockeries have ebbed and waned in popularity over the years, as fashions have changed. There is no doubt that this style of gardening has been greatly influenced by the oriental gardens of China and Japan. In these countries rocks have been used for centuries as major features of the landscape, and the way in which they have been used has been translated easily into the European context.

The main challenge for the gardener constructing a rockery today is to try to create a garden that looks natural and "at one" with the surrounding environment. This requires a good knowledge of how rocks and rocky outcrops appear in their natural state, and an ability to reproduce this look in the garden. A well-planned and well-planted rockery garden is a delight to behold, with contrasting mounds and hummocks of low-growing plants emerging from between the rocks, or cascading over boulders.

PLANTS FOR A PURPOSE

In the broadest sense, rock and alpine gardens are characterized by the use of rocks to create an environment for the cultivation of small and dwarf plants — plants that will thrive in pockets of soil or crevices between the dry, rocky surfaces, with relatively little water. Rock-loving species are found growing wild in virtually every country in the world, and from the widest possible range of climates, soils, altitudes

and conditions. While "true" alpine plants are those that have naturalized in the mountainous zones above the tree line, there are many still classified as alpines that are native to lower mountain slopes and other lowland areas. Certain varieties can easily be moved for cultivation from one country to another, or from a highland to a lowland garden. However, there are still a great many varieties that simply will not travel, and can only be grown successfully in the climate and the soil where they originated.

Luckily, there are plants suitable for every climate, and every situation. In the Mediterranean, for example, many coastal gardens facing the sea are made of rock, with pockets of plants that like warmth and good drainage, and can also tolerate the salty sea air. In southern hemisphere gardens, local native species can be used with great success, again because most prefer built-up beds and well-drained soil. In cool to cold climates, the more traditional approach can be taken, with gently sloping rockery gardens dotted with the "true" alpine plants that like cool winters and short summers.

ROCKERY PLANTS

While it may be true to say that most rockery plants like soil with excellent drainage and at the same time good moisture retention, these requirements can vary considerably from species to species.

LEFT: In a classic scene plants with a low-growing, spreading habit, such as alpine phlox, saxifraga and dwarf conifers, are combined effectively, so that their flowers and foliage textures are complementary.

Many gardeners will not have enough time to learn how to create the precise growing conditions required for each of several temperamental species.

Fortunately, there is now a whole range of plants for rockery gardens that are much easier to cultivate. These plants can be grown successfully in a wide range of soils and climates, and require comparatively little care and attention once established. This is an important consideration, because rock gardens can be a chore to maintain, especially if weeds take hold between the rocks. It really helps to have plants that become quickly established, spreading over the rock surfaces and preventing weeds from becoming a problem.

Plants suitable for rockeries are grouped together for their size and low-growing habit. This type encompasses all those ground-covering and matting plants seen growing on cliffs and rocky slopes in their native environments. Some suitable plants also hail from woodland areas, while others are found clinging to cliffs near the seaside. The varieties that you select for your own garden will be dependent on the climate and soil type where you live, as well as the particular style of rock garden you wish to create.

In general, rockery plants are distinguished by their small leaf size, which helps them to blend in well with the rocky setting. Large-leafed ground-covers are often rampant in growth, and will quickly overwhelm the garden, detracting from the beauty of the rocky outcrops. So, when selecting plants for the rockery garden, look for those that will do well in your district, and that have compact leaves and interesting or bright flowers.

PLANTS FOR THE ALPINE GARDEN

As with any other style of gardening, there are advantages and disadvantages to the building and maintaining of rockeries, and with the cultivation of alpine plants. Purists who specialize only in alpine varieties take infinite trouble to create exactly the right growing conditions for each species. Sometimes the growing of the plant is considered more important than the aesthetics of the garden itself, and great expertise is developed as the gardener learns exactly how each plant species can best be cultivated. In this situation specialized growing environments, such as scree beds, alpine houses or raised beds, are created to provide these very specialized conditions. This style of gardening is seen mainly in the northern hemisphere, where a large number of interesting and unusual alpine varieties are more readily available.

It is sad to realize that until recently alpine plants were not protected from indiscriminate collection, and as a result were often gathered from the wild with little thought for the continuation of individual species. Naturally, some species became extinct, while others became endangered. Fortunately, the situation has changed, and great care is being taken to ensure that some of the rarer plants are protected; they are now carefully cultivated and propagated to ensure their survival.

Traditionally, an alpine garden is one in which the only plants grown are those from the climatic regions above the tree line. The tree line is the area on a mountain slope where trees are found. It ends at the altitude where extremes of cold and wind prevent trees from growing.

Above the tree line is a zone where dwarf trees and shrubs can be found, surviving in pockets of soil and crevices between rocks. Far north, in the Arctic, these growing conditions are actually found at sea level. However, toward the equator, the alpine flora is only seen at high altitudes, often above 10,000ft (3,000m). Obviously, the climate and growing conditions in most gardens are dramatically different from those found in this wild environment, and therefore great trouble has to be taken to ensure the survival of the alpine plants. This may involve creating an artificial environment that will reproduce the natural growing conditions for each particular species.

ALTERNATIVE GROWING ENVIRONMENTS

While the rock garden is the most common setting for the cultivation of alpine and rockery plants, in many cool and cold climates other methods have been devised for creating the most comfortable growing conditions. This is especially true for the cultivation of true alpines. An alpine garden can take many forms, from a rock garden to an above-ground bed, a scree, sink or trough, or an alpine house.

THE SCREE GARDEN

In the wild, mountain rock crumbles as a result of the action of changes in temperature, and exposure to wind and rain. Gradually this crumbled rock slides down the mountain slopes and builds up in sheets behind and between larger rocks and boulders. In this rocky environment, known as scree, the particles of rock vary in size from huge stones down to small

ABOVE: Sinks and troughs provide a controlled growing environment for alpine plants, including excellent drainage. The small scale of the garden makes it possible to keep weeds under control, and also maintain a close watch on the health of individual plants.

RAISED BEDS

This type of growing environment is ideal for any plants that need good drainage, and is also good for gardeners who have difficulty bending or kneeling when tending to the garden. The average raised bed is about 3ft (90cm) in height, and the sides are built up with any good construction material — for example, railway sleepers, timber logs, bricks or stone. If the garden has a sloping area, the built-up bed can take the form of a retaining wall, back-filled with a light, well-drained soil against the slope. To enhance the drainage quality of the raised bed, gravel or small stones can be used at the base, topped with a good soil mix. Both alpine and rockery plants will grow well in this situation, if positioned in a sunny, sheltered situation and tended with care.

CONTAINERS

Sinks and troughs are the best known containers in the world of alpine gardening, although any other kind of large container or tub can also be used if the correct soil and drainage are provided. As many alpine plants are tiny, the containers create the effect of a miniature garden, and this means that a wonderful display can be created on a small scale.

Sinks and troughs are usually discarded stone or slate laundry tubs. If these are not available, concrete or glazed ceramic tubs can be used, often covered with a surface coating such as moss or a mixture of sand, cement and peat that produces a rock-like patina. (see "The Container Garden" in Chapter Two). This surface coating is used purely for visual effect.

fragments and finally to a fine dust. Certain alpine plants thrive in these conditions, sending their long roots deep down into the gravelly bed below.

In the domestic garden, a scree can be created, either as the natural edging of a rock garden, or as a separate growing environment in its own right. In most situations the materials will need to be imported, and mixed together to make an acceptable growing medium. A wide range of raw materials are suitable, including screened clinkers from coal furnaces, fragments and dust from commercial stone quarries, limestone chippings (great for lime-loving plants), clean road base, gravel, and fine river stones. For the garden, these materials are mixed with a light, well-drained loam or garden soil and some peat, if it is available.

THE ALPINE HOUSE

Alpine plants can be grown in pots inside a glasshouse; this will provide them with protection from the rain or winter cold. The alpine house is one way of ensuring a completely controlled growing environment. The temperature will be warm here, but plenty of ventilation must be provided as most alpines resent humidity. The glass walls will block strong winds, and if you water them carefully the plants will not suffer from waterlogged soil conditions.

The alpine house also has the advantage of elevating the plants you grow. Plants are placed on shelves in the alpine house, which allows them to be admired close up. Keen gardeners will often arrange their collections of interesting and unusual plants in a wonderful display. Terracotta pots may be used, on beds of gravel or smooth river stones. This type of display is used primarily to enhance the beauty of the plants.

Whatever method you use for the cultivation of alpine and rockery plants, the pleasure will come from seeing them thrive. And how they thrive will always depend on the growing conditions you provide.

RIGHT: In a glasshouse the temperature, light and air humidity can all be controlled, and of course plants are also protected from damaging winds. Terracotta pots set on gravel beds create exactly the right growing conditions.

STYLE
OPTIONS

The Container Garden

A simple way to enjoy cultivating a wide range of low-growing or alpine plants is to establish a container garden with the correct growing medium. As most of the plants mentioned in this book are compact, they are suitable for growing in pots, tubs, or the more traditional sinks or troughs that are often seen in northern hemisphere gardens.

When planning a container garden, remember that the plants will have the same basic requirements as those grown in a rockery garden. However, there is the added advantage of flexibility, because small container-grown plants can be moved to a more sheltered position when the weather is cold, which is ideal for those gardens in areas that experience heavy rainfall or extreme frosts in winter.

OPPOSITE: Much-loved plants can be displayed in many ways, including sink or trough gardens, or a collection of terracotta pots artistically grouped together. The use of gravel as a ground-cover as well as a mulch, gives unity to the setting.

PREVIOUS PAGE: The stylish use of rocks and plants in a Japanese-style garden can provide inspiration and ideas that can be easily incorporated into a more conventional landscape.

SINKS AND TROUGHS

Sinks and troughs are basically rustic containers used for growing alpine and rockery plants. The concept is to create a miniature landscape in a container with a textured surface that will emulate the stony surface of a rockery where these plants are normally found growing. Old stone troughs, once used in laundries, are sometimes rescued and utilized, as are enamel sinks, which are then coated to give a more textured surface.

It is essential that all containers have adequate drainage holes in the base, and that a deep layer of small stones and pebbles or broken terracotta pots, is used to line the container to provide the right drainage conditions. On top of this layer a polythene membrane should be laid, to prevent the potting soil from going down into the stone layer and becoming clogged. The actual growing medium is a mixture of one part good loam, one part, peat and two parts of coarse grit. To this a good all-purpose fertilizer should be added (a more simple alternative is a good quality potting mix with additional peat and grit added). Sinks and troughs are usually also elevated above ground level on a platform or plinth, again to ensure free drainage and good air circulation. When filled with the soil and drainage layers the trough will be extremely heavy and impossible to move, so make sure you are happy with the final position before filling begins!

SMALL POTS

While in a large container a miniature garden can be created, in smaller pots single specimens only are grown. However, the pots can be arranged in attractive groupings to give a mini-garden effect. When selecting a pot for more sensitive varieties, always opt for one that is porous, such as terracotta. Indeed, this type of pot is generally preferable to plastic, which can hold too much moisture and create either humid or waterlogged conditions. However, remember that terracotta pots will need regular watering, especially in summer, when hot winds can rapidly dry out the potting medium.

Select an open, sunny site for your container garden, but ensure there is protection from strong winds, especially in winter. Avoid overhanging trees and shrubs, which will drip water onto the pots, and line the base with pebbles to create good drainage. As with all container-grown plants, the potting soil is vitally important. Alpines and other varieties that demand perfect drainage should be grown in a mixture that contains both peat and grit, in proportions according to their specific requirements.

ABOVE: A miniature landscape in a large, shallow terracotta container; the soil and rocks mounded to form a small mountain and mulched with gravel, so that even when not in flower, the plants have dramatic effect.

RIGHT: A brilliant splash of brightness with heathers grouped together in rustic pots, combined with an unusual standardized chrysanthemum in full flower.

The Container Garden

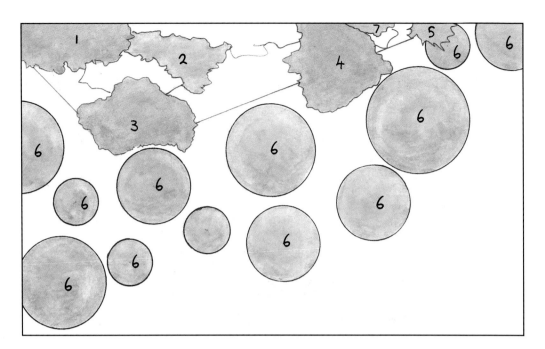

Key to planting

1. *Saxifraga* sp. H. 4in (10cm)
2. *Saxifraga* sp H. 4in (10cm)
3. *Arenaria* sp. H. 4-8in (10-20cm)
4. *Phlox* (alpine) H. 2in (5cm)
5. *Erinus alpinus* H. 2-2 3/4in (5-7cm)
6. *Sempervivum* sp. H. 4-8in (10-20cm)
7. *Dianthus* sp. H. 8-12in (20-30cm)

Creating a display garden with containers is a relatively easy way to enjoy the pleasure of growing these delightful small plants in a garden that might otherwise not be suitable, due to size or orientation. The aim is to recreate exactly the same growing environment that the plants normally experience in their natural habitat, by siting the garden in a sunny but sheltered situation, and ensuring that the soil mixes are well drained but capable of holding sufficient moisture for the plants to thrive even in warm or hot weather. Select plants that have similar growing requirements, and that blend together well in size, shape, and foliage texture.

The Japanese Garden

In Japanese landscape design the studied use of rocks is the most powerful element. While plants have an important part in the overall design and shape of the garden, it is the rocks that form the basic framework around which the garden is then constructed. Often rocks are used in a natural fashion, so that the completed scene exactly represents one particular aspect of nature.

While the Japanese garden is not a traditional setting for the growing of alpine or rockery plants, it is certainly worth considering as a garden feature, just for the beautiful way in which the rocks are used. Small plants such as dwarf conifers and miniature weeping maples can be used effectively, and interesting foliage plants integrated into the framework of rocks.

Once established, a Japanese-style garden should require a minimum of maintenance, which is ideal for busy people who do not have time to tend a rockery garden. Many of the plants are evergreen or foliage plants, and this gives the garden a simplicity that is very appealing.

ELEMENTS OF DESIGN

A traditional Japanese garden is quite specific in design, and purists will be critical of amateur attempts at emulating this style of landscaping. Simply by incorporating a Japanese lantern or bamboo fountain, you will not automatically make the garden "Japanese", however it is quite possible to capture some of the feeling and atmosphere with the clever use of rocks and water. In essence the style is very simple and subtle, although usually a great amount of time has been spent just placing the rocks sympathetically. Never stand rocks on their sides or at unnatural angles, instead try to create a scene that looks completely settled into the environment. Aged and mossy rocks that are covered with lichen, especially when used near water, will add to the atmosphere.

Brightly coloured foliage and flowers are to be avoided, except for the brilliant autumn foliage of the maple, which is usually used as an accent or edging plant near ponds or lakes. Other plants commonly used include bamboo (*Bambusa* sp.), cotoneasters, camellias, shapely conifers, red and black pines (*Pinus* sp.), cedars (*Cedrus* sp.), and a variety of rushes and sedges. Waterlilies can be grown as deep water plants, but only in ponds that receive enough sunshine.

Bridges, spanning small streams or ponds, are also seen as a symbol of Japanese garden style. These should be gently arched and of a simple design, linking two areas of the garden rather than standing out as a design feature in their own right. If painting a timber bridge use subtle colours, such as soft greens and greys.

LEFT: The structural elements of a Japanese garden are always simple, and this is what gives it such timeless appeal. Here a fascinating collection of unusually shaped rocks have been combined effectively, set in a bed of gravel and framed by a few outstanding plants. Flower colour is not a major factor in the design, although small trees are sometimes chosen for their spring blossom or autumn tonings.

The Japanese Garden

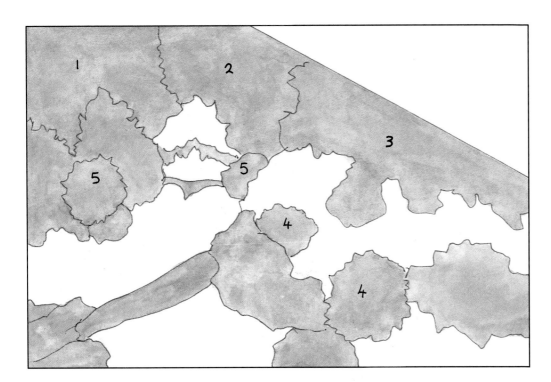

Key to planting

1. *Camellia japonica* H. to 20ft (7m)
2. *Camellia sasanqua* H. to 9ft (3m)
3. *Pinus thunbergii* H. 30ft (10m)
4. *Azalea kurume* 'white' H. to 4ft (1.5m)
5. *Azalea kurume* 'pink' H. to 4ft (1.5m)

Although not a traditional setting for the cultivation of alpine or rockery plants, a Japanese-style garden is one in which the use of rock is a predominant feature. As a departure from the traditional rockery garden, where brightly coloured plants fill every space between the rocks, a Japanese garden relies more on the outline shape of the trees and shrubs, as well as the shape of the rocks and the way in which they are set into the landscape. In this scheme the strong horizontal lines of the tree branches contrast with the large chunks of textured stone, while plants have been chosen for the beauty of their foliage as much as their flowers.

The Scree Garden

In nature, screes are areas on the sides of mountains where rocks have crumbled due to the extremes of climate. Screes occur when intense heat, cold or rain cause large boulders to crack and break down into much smaller fragments. As the land where screes are found is generally sloping, these rock fragments slide downwards with the forces of gravity, and accumulate in sheets or pockets against larger rocks.

The scree is composed of fragments that range in size from quite large stones down to fine dust, providing an ideal growing environment for a wide range of plants that seem to thrive in these conditions. Although this phenomenon is largely confined to alpine regions, similar growing conditions can also be found in lowland areas, in gravelly areas beside rivers and streams, or in shingle that is found near the sea. Again, these areas provide a good growing medium for a variety of plants that can also be grown in a domestic garden.

OPPOSITE: One of the most attractive alpine or rockery features for the garden is the scree bed, which emulates the rocky, free-draining soil conditions found on the sides of mountains. This style allows for the growing of a wide range of plants that insist on perfect drainage, and send their roots deep into the scree mixture for nutrients.

MATERIALS

Re-creating a scree in your garden is not difficult; however it may require bringing in a lot of raw materials in the form of stone chippings and gravel. There are many combinations of ingredients, and the final selection will be based upon what is readily available, and not too expensive, in your local area. Sometimes quarries have accumulated piles of dust and rock fragments that can be used for the purpose, mixed with larger rocks and some good loam and peat that will provide the actual growing medium. A basic recipe is three parts gravel and stone to one part loam and one part peat. This provides a good balance of textures, and will form the basis of the scree garden.

CONSTRUCTION

Siting a scree garden will depend on the existing landscape. Often screes are introduced as the edging of a rockery garden, helping it to blend into the surrounding garden, and preventing lawn from invading the rockery. If possible, the scree should be on a sloping site, to make it appear more natural, and to ensure that water can run off easily after rain or watering. Like a rockery garden, it should be located in an open, sunny position with good air circulation, but protected from strong winds. If there are drainage problems in the soil beneath the scree, these must be corrected before the garden is constructed. Sharp sand can be dug into clay soil as a foundation, or underground plastic drainage pipes laid to take the water away.

The same basic preparation for creating a rockery is necessary for a scree bed. All traces of lawn and lawn runners or perennial weeds must be cleared from the area before the scree bed is laid. A 2in (5cm) deep layer of sand is a good basis upon which to lay the scree mixture, which should at least 9in (20cm) deep. When the scree is in position, it should be watered well to settle the ingredients before planting out.

PLANTING

Most of the plants grown in screes are those difficult high alpine varieties that demand critical drainage. Cushion or mat-forming plants are the most effective, as they will probably grow and spread to cover the scree surface. When planting, make sure that the plant roots come into contact with some soil, adding extra compost/peat mixture around the root ball. When first planted regular watering is important, as the young plant's roots need to spread down through the scree in search of moisture.

The Scree Garden

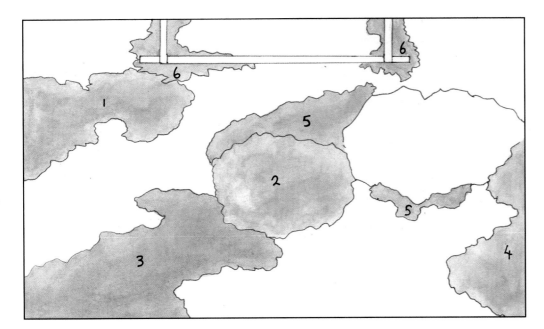

Key to planting

1. *Genista* sp. H. 3ft (1m)
2. *Euryops* sp. H. 1ft (30cm)
3. *Adonis vernalis* H. 1ft (30cm)
4. *Dionysia tapetodes* H. 2in (5cm)
5. *Androsace* sp. H. 4in (10cm)
6. *Vitis* sp. (ornamental grapes)

A scree bed can be created in any garden, generally best sited where a naturally gentle slope will assist with the run off of water beneath the rocky surface. Often scree beds are used to edge a rockery or alpine bed, to help it visually blend in with the rest of the garden. The scree material needs to be at least 9in (20cm) deep, and should consist of a blend of rock chips, gravel, and a moisture-retentive soil mix. When planting in a scree, always ensure that the plant roots have some contact with the soil mix, to help them become established.

The Low-Profile Bed

This planting design, also known as a flat outcrop bed, is very effective in a garden without natural slopes or contours suitable for the construction of a major rockery garden. In simple terms, it is a flat or slightly sloping bed into which stones of various size have been arranged in the most natural way possible. Between the rocks, plants are established with a view to filling all the gaps, and eventually overlapping the stones to tie the entire bed together.

Most low-profile beds are laid out in an informal fashion, with softly curved or rounded edges. Rock material that is selected carefully will sit comfortably into position. The most commonly used stone is either sandstone or limestone, although other types can be used if readily available in your area.

OPPOSITE: This charming bed, surrounded by lawn, demonstrates how effectively alpines and rockery plants can be grown in this informal situation. Unlike a rockery, which involves a lot of construction, the low-profile bed is easily laid out in soil that is well drained, using local rock between plants.

PREPARATION

As with any garden bed that uses rock, careful preparation must be made to ensure that perennial weeds or grass runners do not get in and around the stones. Avoid using herbicides to clear the area; instead try lifting as many weeds as possible, then mulching with a thick layer of newspapers that will suppress further weed growth. Once again, good drainage is also vital. Dig a hole to the depth of 1ft (30cm) and fill with water, allowing it then to sit for several hours. If the water has not drained away, it is an indication that the subsoil is a heavy clay and will require breaking down to improve drainage. Add gypsum, or incorporate plenty of organic matter to correct the problem.

When laying out the stones remember that uniformity is not always necessary. Indeed, selecting stones of differing sizes and shapes will create a more visually interesting bed, though none of them should be huge boulders which will destroy the low-growing feeling of the garden. Examine each stone as you lay it, looking for the most interesting surface to expose, then position it firmly into place, so that it will not move when walked upon. When planting and maintaining the garden this framework of stones will be used as "stepping stones", so they must be solid under foot.

PLANTING

The soil between the rocks will probably need to be improved upon prior to planting. A light mixture that also holds moisture is preferable, and this can be achieved by mixing together a light, sandy loam with some peat moss and well-matured compost. Plants can either be planted as the bed is being constructed, or later when the stones are all in their positions.

Try to combine different foliage textures and flower colours together, so that the plants complement each other, and also provide colour over as many months of the year as possible. The type of plants used will depend on the prevailing climate and conditions, although in cooler areas a low-profile bed is considered an excellent way of growing many of the more difficult cushion-forming alpines. However, this style will also work equally well in more temperate climates, as an environment for low-growing coastal or Mediterranean plants.

After planting, mulch around plants with gravel or a coarse grit that will not only prevent weeds from becoming established, but will also help to bind the rocks and plants together visually. Water the plants well, and keep the water up to them until they become well established.

The Low-Profile Bed

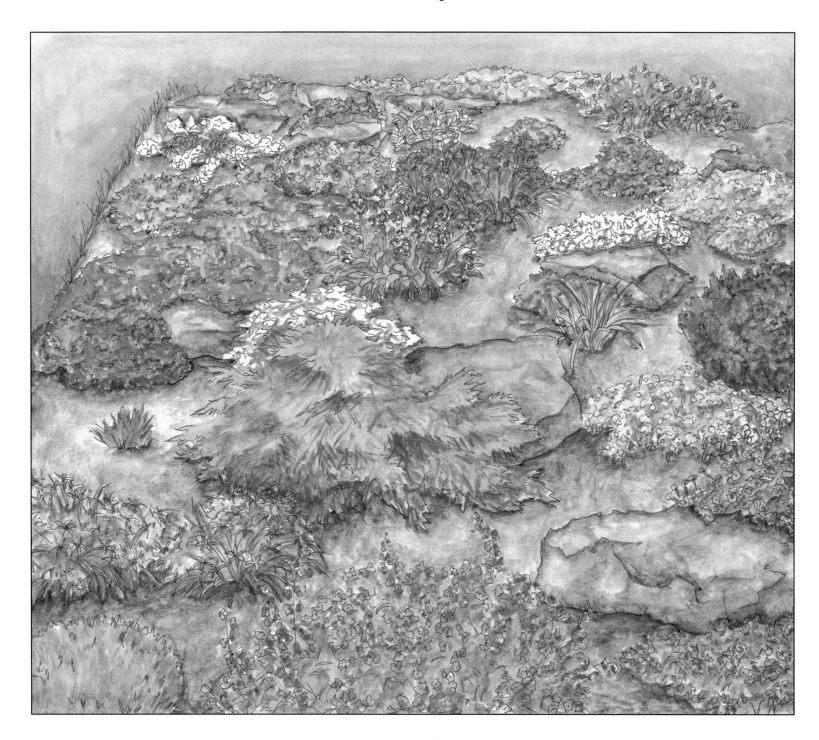

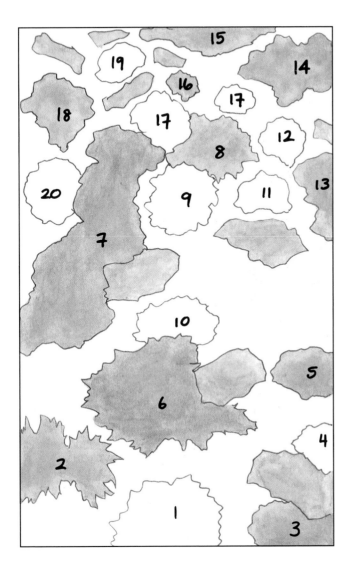

Key to planting

1. *Campanula* sp. H. 1ft (30cm)
2. *Ipheion uniflorum* H. 6in (15cm)
3. *Anagallis monelli* H.4in (10cm)
4. *Gentiana acaulis* H. 3in (8cm)
5. *Geum montanum* H. 5in (12cm)
6. *Juniperus communis* 'Depressa Aurea'
   H. 20in (50cm)
7. *Phlox* (alpine) H. 2in (5cm)
8. *Armeria* sp. H. 10in (25cm)
9. *Primula* sp. H. 1ft (30cm)
10. *Arenaria montana* H. 8in (20cm)
11. *Anemone baldensis* H. 4in (10cm)
12. *Androsace alpina* H. 1in (2.5cm)
13. *Lithospermum* sp. H. 6in (15cm)
14. *Soldanella alpina.* H. 4in (10cm)
15. *Hypericum olympicum* H. 10in (25cm)
16. *Salix reticulata* H. 1in (2.5cm)
17. *Geranium dalmaticum* H. H. 2in (5cm)
18. *Saxifraga longiflora* H. 2ft (60cm)
19. *Campanula* sp. H. 6in (15cm)
20. *Campanula* sp. H. 1ft (30cm)

A low-profile bed is a simple landscaping style for growing a wide range of small, ground-covering plants without the necessity of constructing an elaborate rockery garden. The main site requirement is excellent drainage, because the plants will be positioned directly in the ground, not into pockets of specially prepared soil as in a rockery. Select a sunny, open position, and test the soil drainage before incorporating rocks or plants. Select plants that will grow well in your climate and soil type, avoiding the more sensitive species that require perfect drainage.

The Miniature Garden

One of the most delightful ways of growing alpine and small rockery plants is in a miniature garden, which provides a wonderful showcase for these tiny plants. The miniature garden is ideal for people with little or no garden space, or who live in a climate that is too harsh for a conventional rockery garden.

Most alpine and rockery plants are small and low growing, generally with tiny leaves and dainty flowers. This makes them perfect for planting in a scaled-down garden, that can include small rocks for texture and height variation. Container gardens are often planted in this way, and you will see charming sinks and troughs that have been planted out with dwarf conifers and a range of low-growing and cascading alpines to create a miniature "scene". This style of planting can be carried over into small raised beds or even trays on a platform that are easy for maintaining (no bending necessary) and for close-up inspection of the plants. A miniature garden is an achievable way of enjoying the pleasures of growing unusual or sensitive plants, without undertaking the huge task of laying out and maintaining a rockery garden. It can be restricted to just two or three different species of plants, which can be tended in this relatively controlled environment.

PREPARATION

However it is designed, the miniature garden will need the same basic environment as all rockery and alpine beds. The site should be open and sunny, away from overhanging trees and shrubs that will drip water onto the plants and rocks. Protection should be provided against strong winds, which is the reason that small courtyards are very practical for this particular style. In cold climates, winter protection against frost and icy rain will also be required, but the size of the garden should ensure that this is not a problem. A simple frame that allows the warmth of the winter sun to penetrate, but keeps out cold winds and

ABOVE: Pretty as a picture, this small raised bed has been planted as a miniature garden, with a variety of hardy rockery plants including ajuga and campanula, that will cascade over the edges of the stone framework.

rain, will help the garden survive the worst of the weather.

Determining the size of the garden will allow for precise preparation of the growing environment. Establish which particular plants you wish to grow, then set about creating the perfect conditions. Rocks can be incorporated into the scene, but they must remain within the overall scale of the garden. Look for small, weathered rocks with interesting surface patterns and textures, and position them around the bed with sufficient space between them for the plants. Naturally, good drainage is important, and this can be achieved by building in a drainage layer at the base, as is done in a container (sink or trough). Broken terracotta tiles or stones can be placed at the base of the garden, with a polythene membrane layer to prevent the soil mixture from washing down and clogging up the drainage material.

PLANTING

Once again, a good soil mixture is vital to the success of the garden. Mix together a light, sandy loam with some peat moss and well-matured compost. Add more grit if the plants selected require sharp drainage. In a raised or platform bed, select plants for the edges that will softly cascade or trail over the sides, and more compact, mound-forming plants for the centre of the garden. Avoid any plants with large leaves, as this is a sure sign that they will grow quite large and probably spread, overwhelming other, more delicate, plants in the garden. Water well after planting, and mulch to prevent annual weed seeds from taking root.

ABOVE: This delightful rectangular garden forms a miniature scene, complete with background "trees" and a mixed planting of brilliant alpines and rockery specimens. Note how the contrasting tones of foliage are just as dramatic as the flowers in the bed.

The Miniature Garden

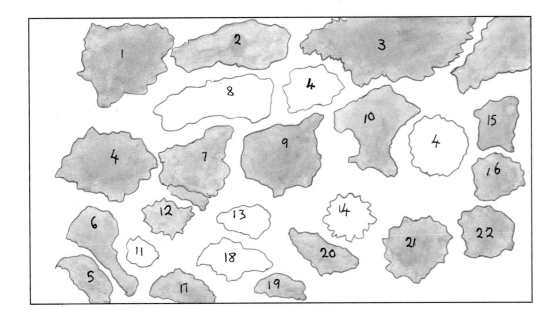

Key to planting

1. *Chamaecyparis obtusa* 'Pygmaea'
   H. 1 3/4ft (50cm)
2. *Linum arboreum* H. to 1ft (30cm)
3. *Chamaecyparis obtusa* 'Nana' H. to 2ft (60cm)
4. *Dianthus deltoides* H. 6in (15cm)
5. *Dianthus deltoides* H. 6in (15cm)
6. *Phlox hoodii* H. 2in (5cm)
7. *Saxifraga scardica* H. 1in (2-3cm)
8. *Saxifraga* 'Jenkinsiae' H. 4in (10cm)
9. *Dionysia tapeodes* H. 4in (10cm)
10. *Gentiana acaulis* H. 4in (10cm)
11. *Phlox* 'Camla' H. 4in (10cm)
12. *Gentiana verna* H. 2in (5cm)
13. *Azorella trifurcata* H. 4in (10cm)
14. *Armeria pseudarmeria* H. 1ft (30cm)
15. *Dionysia aretioides* H. 2in (5cm)
16. *Sanguinaria canadensis* H. 4in (10cm)
17. *Arenaria purpurascens* H. 1in (2cm)
18. *Saxifraga oppositifolia* H. 1in (2cm)
19. *Antennaria dioica* 'Rosea' H. 1 1/2in (3cm)
20. *Saxifraga moschata* H. 4in (10cm)
21. *Campanula cochleariifolia* H. 3in (8cm)
22. *Polygala calcarea* H. 1in (2cm)

In spite of its small size, this miniature garden manages to accommodate more than 20 species of plants that have been carefully chosen for their compact growth habit, and small leaf size. The bed is raised only 10in (20cm) above a gravel bed, to ensure good drainage. The garden itself is also mulched with gravel, to keep weeds down and to prevent ground-level humidity, which can occur when organic matter is used as a mulch. Dwarf conifers at the back of the bed give height to the scene, while ground-hugging varieties are interplanted with species that carry their flowers on stems above the plant.

The Water Rockery

This is yet another variation on the theme of rockery gardening. In many situations, it is appropriate for water to be introduced into the landscape, as a major feature or as an integrated part of the rockery. As many water gardens are edged with rocks, it seems ideal that the entire surrounds can be constructed as rockery gardens, with excellent results.

In general, the plants grown in rockery gardens demand excellent drainage and resent "wet feet", which will occur at the edges of naturally formed streams and ponds. However, in a man-made water garden the surrounds will generally be quite dry and capable of supporting the type of plants mentioned in this book.

As a feature in the garden, water is difficult to surpass. Whether it is a still pond or lake, or a trickling waterfall or stream, the presence of water brings an added dimension and mood in every situation. In these days of low-voltage submersible pumps and heavy duty rubber pool liners, it is possible to construct a wonderful water garden with a minimum of expense and effort, and create an ideal environment for the growing of a wide range of interesting and unusual plants. The way in which the edges and sides of the water garden are treated, will greatly determine just how natural it appears within the context of the garden. Most gardeners try to soften the impact with rocks and plants, and this in turn lends itself to growing those plants that thrive in the cracks and crannies between rocks.

When combining water features and rockery gardens, keep in mind that moving water may splash the sides of the stream or waterfall, and create very damp, and humid conditions that will not suit many alpine or rockery species. Birds are also attracted to water, and they can send water flying in all directions, especially when taking a bath. Therefore select plants for the edges of the pool that can withstand a little moisture, siting the more sensitive species further away from the water. Choose bright and colourful plants, that will throw reflections onto the water's surface, as this reflective quality is a major part of the attraction of water gardens.

CONSTRUCTION AND PLANTING

When planning and planting a rockery with water features, the same basic construction principles apply. Choose a sunny, open position and ensure that the ground beneath the rockery has excellent drainage. The rocks used around edges of the pond, or down the sides of the waterfall, should overlap so that the lining material is not visible. Use edging plants that will cascade over these rocks, to soften the edges, and consider incorporating some water plants both in the deep water and along the margins of the pool to provide a link between the water and the rockery garden. Waterlilies are ideal, and they also enjoy the open, sunny conditions required by rockeries. If the pond is still, plant some oxygenating species that will help keep the water healthy and prevent algal growth in summer.

OPPOSITE: A wonderful combination of rocks, water and plants that have been used together in a neat and well-designed rockery garden that incorporates several water features. A small formal fountain feeds water into a controlled stream that flows down to a larger holding pond, flagged by stone.

The Water Rockery

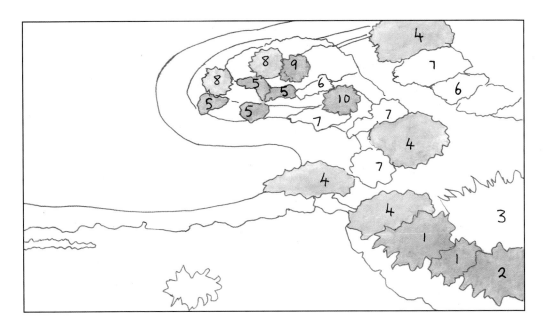

Key to planting

1. *Hosta* sp. H. 2ft (60cm)
2. *Hosta* sp. H. 2 1/2ft (75cm)
3. *Iris* sp. H. 3ft (90cm)
4. *Campanula* sp. H. 1ft (30cm)
5. *Phlox* (alpine) H. 2in (5cm)
6. *Phlox* (alpine) H. 2in (5cm)
7. *Alyssum* sp.H. 2in (5cm)
8. *Thuja orientalis* 'Aurea Nana' H. 2ft (60cm)
9. *Thuja orientalis* 'Rosedalis' H. 5ft (1.5m)
10. *Juniperus communis* "Compressa'
    H. 2 1/2ft (75cm)

A water feature can be successfully built into a rockery garden if there are controls to ensure that the moisture does not affect the health of the plants. Although the land in this garden is basically flat, the rockery has been elevated to a point where the fountain forms the central feature, then feeding a stream that trickles gently through the individual planting beds, which are well drained because of their elevation. The sides of the stream and the edges of the pond have been softened with cascading plants, chosen to withstand the odd splash of water that these conditions will create.

The Raised Bed

Raised beds provide excellent drainage, which is one of the main prerequisites of growing alpines, and most rockery plants. In many situations, a raised bed is more practical than a rockery, for reasons of space or design. In courtyards and small gardens where a rockery would appear out of scale, and out of place, a raised bed can provide a good growing environment for a wide range of plants. Raised beds are also ideal for gardens with heavy clay soil or other drainage problems that can sometimes make a rockery garden totally impractical.

Apart from improving soil drainage, raised beds are also ideal for gardeners who have difficulty bending or kneeling for long periods. They bring the plants up to eye level, where they can be really appreciated. Many gardeners feel they have more control over the growing environment in a raised bed, and as a result they have a greater success with the more sensitive and difficult species that can get lost in a traditional rockery garden.

SITING AND CONSTRUCTION

Position the raised bed in a sunny but sheltered place, away from trees and shrubs. Against a sunny wall is an ideal position, although in summer this will create very warm growing conditions, and therefore extra watering may be required. Dappled shade is acceptable, however, if any of the shade-loving varieties are being cultivated. Depending on the size of the bed, it could even be positioned half in full sun, and half in semi-shade to that both growing conditions are provided.

The elevation of a raised bed can vary from 1ft (30cm) to 3ft (90cm), according to the situation. Retaining walls any higher than this can be unstable, and there is always a risk of collapse under the weight of the growing medium (especially after heavy rain) unless they have been professionally built. In some areas local authorities need to be notified, and will inspect, any retaining walls more than 3ft (1m) in height, and this should be checked prior to construction.

The construction material for the sides of a raised bed varies considerable. In a formal rectangular or square bed, timber or brick construction is often used, while in less formal gardens rock or stone can be the materials used for the construction of the sides. Stone certainly has the most natural appearance, and will complement the plants in the same way as when used in a rockery garden. All styles of retaining wall will require provision for water drainage at various points along the sides, especially near the base. It is important that water is never allowed to accumulate at the back of the wall, firstly because the plants will greatly resent these waterlogged conditions, and secondly because this will place pressure on the wall itself.

FILLING AND PLANTING

Think of the raised bed as a large container. Just as the base of a pot is lined with a coarse fill to improve drainage, so the base of the raised bed must be backfilled with broken terracotta tiles or stones to create a free-draining foundation. Once again, the growing medium must be light, yet capable of holding moisture. A mix of good loam, grit, and peat will serve this purpose, with a handful of bonemeal to get plants off to a good start. Rocks can be set into the soil surface, providing they are in scale with the size of the garden, and plants arranged in between them. Select trailing plants for the edges, and larger species for the back of the bed.

OPPOSITE: This solid brick retaining wall, approximately 3ft (1m) in height, has been backfilled with rich but well-drained soil mix, into which a variety of low-growing shrubs, conifers and bulbs have been planted.

The Raised Bed

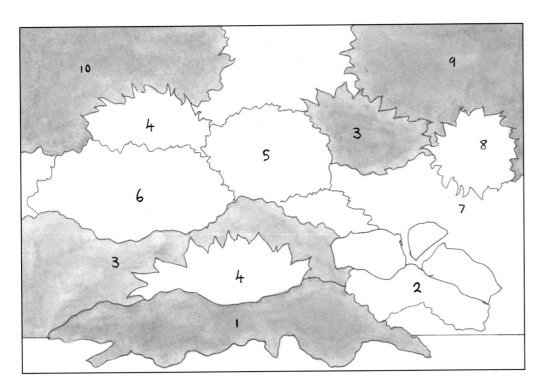

Key to planting

1. *Alyssum saxatile* H. 8in (20cm)
2. *Cardamine pratensis* H. 10in (25cm)
3. *Tulipa* 'white' H. 18in (45cm)
4. *Tulipa* 'red' H. 18in (45cm)
5. *Campanula portenschlagiana* H. 6in (15cm)
6. *Erica cinerea* H. 1ft (30cm)
7. *Andromeda polifolia* H. 1ft (30cm)
8. *Fritillaria imperialis* H. 10in (25cm)
9. *Rhododendron* sp. H. 6ft (2m)
10. *Azalea* sp. H. 4 1/2ft (1.5m)

The raised bed in this design has been taken to the full height of 3ft (1m) with drainage holes at the base to allow free run off of water, even after heavy rainfall. The plants chosen for this situation can vary according to taste, from true alpines or rockery plants, to a variety of low-growing shrubs, conifers, bulbs, and perennials that will enjoy the free-draining conditions provided. The sides of a raised bed can be made from brick or stone, either laid formally or as a drystone wall; or timber in the form of treated timber logs or recycled railway sleepers. The soil used to backfill the retaining wall should be adjusted according to the plants featured, with added grit if alpines or rockery plants are being used.

The Sloping Bed

A sloping site can be used for growing alpine and rockery plants, without necessarily being constructed as a full-scale or elaborate rockery garden. In some gardens there are naturally sloping areas that are well drained, because water runs down the sides of the embankment and away from plant roots. This creates a good growing environment for many of the plants listed in this book.

In any garden, variations of level are an excellent way of creating an interesting planting feature. Gardens with this built-in advantage also give the illusion of being larger, because part of the garden is out of sight. Just how they are planted will greatly depend on the climate and soil type, and the orientation (direction in which the slope is facing).

THE SHADY SLOPE

If the naturally sloping area of the garden is facing away from the sun, or is shaded by overhanging trees and shrubs, this

OPPOSITE: A natural slope is the ideal situation for growing all kinds of plants that prefer good drainage. This pretty pathway that leads from one level of the garden to the next, has been planted out with a mixture of rockery specimens, succulents and ornamental grasses.

will affect the type of plants that can be grown. Most alpine and rockery species prefer sunny conditions, however there still quite a few that will thrive in more sheltered and shady situations. Woodland plants, accustomed to growing beneath a canopy of taller trees, can be established in this situation, providing the correct soil conditions are provided. Woodland plants must have plenty of leaf mould and peat in the soil, as these are the conditions in which they are naturally found. Plants such as Ramonda, Primula, Vaccinium, and Crocus will thrive on a shady slope that has been enriched with plenty of peat and mulched with leaf mould. They enjoy these rich, moist conditions, but will resent waterlogged soil, so make sure that there is adequate drainage beneath the topsoil layer.

THE SUNNY SLOPE

Where plenty of sun is available, the choice of plants is much more flexible. The major problem will be holding the soil on the slope, because there is a tendency for light, sandy topsoils to wash away in heavy rain. It may be necessary to create terraces down the side of the embankment, depending on the angle of the slope. Large rocks are obviously the best choice for this

purpose, as they can be bedded into the soil and will prevent landslides from occurring. The roots of the plants, too, will help to bind the sloping site together, but it will take time until they are well established. In the meantime, it may be necessary to use some fine wire mesh to hold the soil and plants in place. Temporary rocks can also be used as a firming mulch, and later removed when the plant roots have taken over.

If the area of slope leads from one part of the garden to another, steps may be necessary, and these can be made into a delightful feature. The soil around the steps should be improved with the addition of well-matured compost and peat, plus some grit if the plants to be used here require sharp drainage. Encourage plants to nestle into the edges of the steps, but take care not to use vigorous growers that will take over, and block easy passage up and down the steps or pathway.

Where there is only a gentle slope, a shingle path can be created by laying gravel or small rock particles, similar to those used in a scree bed. The edges of this path can be planted with rockery plants and alpines that enjoy these particular growing conditions, and this will create a wonderful effect.

The Sloping Bed

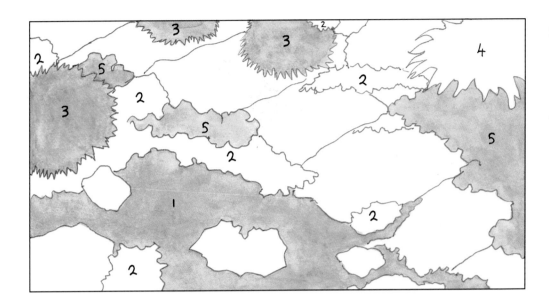

Key to planting

1. *Sedum* sp. H. 1ft (30cm)
2. *Androsace* sp. H. 4in (10cm)
3. *Fetusca* sp. H. 1ft (30cm)
4. *Agapanthus* sp. H. 3ft (1m)
5. *Echeveria* sp. H. 2in (4cm)

Use sloping land to great effect, as it is one of the strongest assets in the garden. When there is more than one level it creates an impression of spaciousness, and gives the gardener scope for landscaping hidden corners and small scenes that create surprises when you walk from one area to the next. Here a pathway has been constructed through a naturally sloping rockery, using concrete steps and a surrounding of plants that have interesting and unusual foliage in a variety of textures. Care has been taken not to use invasive species next to the steps, as this may make walking more difficult if the plants are allowed to take over.

DESIGNING & BUILDING ROCK GARDENS

Designed to last

The rock garden offers every gardener scope for individual creativity. To do justice to your own creative ideas, take great care with planning and executing all major landscaping features in the garden. This will ensure that they stand the test of time, and will give the plants you choose the best opportunity for thriving.

In Victorian gardens, rockeries were sometimes designed to look like miniature mountain landscapes, complete with artificial, "snow-capped" peaks. In today's garden, this could be considered rather over the top! Instead, most rock gardens now aim to emulate nature, and to look as though they have been part of the site forever. For this purpose, study what is already there before deciding on what to bring in to your garden. If there are large boulders and rocks on the site, for example, study their position carefully before you

OPPOSITE: This carefully constructed terraced rockery has deep pockets of well-prepared soil that will suit the cultivation of a wide range of species with a diverse range of growing requirements.

PREVIOUS PAGE: The aim of good rockery construction is to provide a solid, lasting framework as a background to establishing the correct growing conditions for each individual plant, such as these healthy Erinus alpinus.

move them away, and draw a rough plan showing where they are in the garden.

Time taken to draw a design for your garden is time well invested. A design on paper will help to give a clear idea of the outline of your rock garden, and the approximate size and shape of the rocks that will be required. It also may be useful to draw a ground plan of your entire garden, and to include a scale-size outline of the rockery, to see how comfortably it will sit in relation to the size of the land and other major existing features, such as the house and established trees and shrubs. It is important that the rockery fits well into the landscape, and does not overpower or overwhelm other features. Keep it in scale with the rest of your garden. A very large rock garden will also be difficult to maintain, and require an enormous amount of planting.

Ideally, your rock garden should blend in with the existing garden, and this can only be achieved by careful siting and planning. Take photographs of the proposed site, and then, on an overlay of tracing paper, sketch the approximate design and location of your planned rockery. Then you will be able to see it in relationship to the rest of the garden.

Consider the shape of your garden, so that the rockery can be designed to be an outstanding feature. If the garden is square, or has many angles where the lawn meets

garden beds, perhaps a sweeping circular or oval rockery will have the desired softening effect. As a sloping site is more natural, keep in mind that this will add height to the garden, which in turn will give an added feeling of spaciousness. The low-growing plants used in the rockery will certainly contrast well with taller growing trees and shrubs seen in distant vistas. The textured surface of the rocks, too, will provide a striking contrast to plain areas of lawn.

Also give some thought to how the rockery edges will be phased into the surrounding garden. Lawn running up to the sides can be a problem, as it may invade the soil around the rocks. Some rockery gardens are edged with scree or gravel, which visually eases the whole structure into the landscape and keeps the grass at bay.

SELECTING A SITE

There are several major factors to consider when you choose a suitable location for the rock garden. Always keep in mind that the garden you are building must provide the appropriate growing environment for rockery and alpine plants. In general, these plants will only thrive in very free-draining soils, sometimes even gravel or scree, and so this must be considered at all stages of construction.

Apart from needing good drainage, most of the plants used in a rockery also like

ABOVE: A garden of this size is a major undertaking, and provides scope for growing brightly coloured perennials with range of rockery plants that will survive the rather open, exposed conditions.

OPPOSITE: Although rock is a major feature in the design of the garden, its impact can be greatly softened by selecting plants that spread and sprawl, covering the soil pockets and visually binding the structure together.

plenty of sun and free movement of air in order to grow successfully — begin by looking for the most open, sunny place in the garden. But, while free air movement is important, exposure to strong prevailing winds is not desirable, so ensure that some wind protection is provided, in the form of a hedge, wall or windbreak.

Avoid positioning your rockery or alpine garden beneath or adjacent to over-hanging trees, as this will create several major problems. Firstly, after rainfall the dripping water from the trees above will cause a lot of ground-level moisture,

which is resented by many rock and alpine garden species. Secondly, the shady conditions beneath trees are unsuitable for a wide range of plants; while one corner of your rock garden may be in the shade so that you can grow those particular varieties that like semi-shade, the major part of the rock garden should have as much sun as possible.

Lastly, the roots from large trees and shrubs will invade the rockery, competing for soil moisture and nutrients. When the garden is watered the roots of surrounding plants will naturally travel upwards in

search of moisture. Once these roots have become entangled with the rocks, the plants you have positioned in the small pockets of soil throughout the rock garden will soon stop thriving. So the ideal site for your design is an open, sunny position that is sheltered from strong winds and positioned well away from trees and large shrubs.

In cool to cold climates, where alpine plants can be grown in your rock garden, avoid cool hollows where frosts will gather in late winter or early spring. Also test the soil at ground level for adequate drainage. Although the rock garden will be built above ground level, any excess wetness or lack of drainage can affect plants during prolonged rainy weather. In the worst situation, the pockets of soil between the rocks will become water-logged, and this will be fatal to a great many species. If you find drainage is poor on your proposed site, consider either selecting an alternative site, or installing underground drainage pipes to take moisture away from the soil surface.

Aesthetics is another important factor when choosing the site. You are fortunate if there is an existing slope on the land, as this is the most natural-looking area for a rock garden, and the most suitable environment for the placement of rocks. On a completely flat block of land it may be necessary to import rubble or organic fill to create a higher level or slope where the rockery is to be positioned. However, it is possible to create an attrac-tive and natural-looking rockery on flat ground, providing the rocks are care-fully and thoughtfully placed and the planting is in sympathy with the rest of the surroundings.

MATERIALS FOR THE ROCK GARDEN

Another important aspect of design is the materials you use for your rock garden. The selection of stone or rock for the construction of a rock garden is of primary importance, as this material will be the dominant element of the garden and one over which you have total control; whereas the other vital element, the soil, will be far more dependent on the prevailing conditions in your garden.

SELECTING ROCKS AND STONES

Use local rock wherever possible, for several good reasons. Rock that has been quarried or gathered nearby will be less expensive, because it will not require long-distance transport. Local rock will also blend in well with the local environment, because it will be in harmony with the surroundings, its tones matching the native soil and any existing rocky outcrops nearby. Also, if there are quarry or landscape supply yards with large supplies of rock close to home, you will have the opportunity to view the rock. Then you will be able to select individual pieces that can be used as features, determining the size, shape and surface texture or grain of the pieces you require, rather than having an unknown selection of rock delivered to your garden gate.

Avoid mixing two or more rock types in the garden, as this will look unconvincing. In nature, the local stone reflects the local soil type, and you will never find a mixture of rock types in one small region. Look for roughly textured rocks that have not been split or otherwise damaged, as this will

ABOVE: Ultimately, it is the contrast of texture between rock and plant that will create the most lasting effect. Here the delicate, feather foliage of the Japanese maple (Acer palmatum) *stands out against the solid texture of a large rock slab.*

OPPOSITE: Use stone that is readily available in your immediate area, not simply because it is less expensive, but also because it will blend in better with the local soil and environment.

spoil their natural surface appearance. Some of the softer stone varieties, such as sandstone, may not be suitable in regions where the winter temperatures are very low. This is because the stone is porous and will absorb water, which may lead to cracking and crumbling if there is a sudden drop in overnight temperatures.

In most climates, stone that has a natural stratification, such as limestone, will give the most aesthetic results. However, be aware that limestone will leach a small quantity of lime into the soil — this is acceptable if the plants you use are suited to alkaline soil (most alpine varieties prefer these conditions). Acid-loving species — rhododendrons are an example — will not be suited to this particular soil environment.

Granite is an excellent choice, but it is very dense and weighty, and can be a chore to move around. Basalt and other volcanic rocks are also heavy, although they often have an interesting and unusual pitted surface texture that can look most effective. Shale and slate can also be used if available, although some types may deteriorate when exposed to harsh weather over long periods. Ask for some expert advice from your landscape supplier or nursery before buying stone, to determine its lasting qualities.

ABOVE: *In many gardens the soil will need to be improved by the addition of plenty of organic matter, and in certain situations grit or sand will be necessary to create sharp drainage for those plants that demand these growing conditions.*

MODIFYING YOUR GARDEN SOIL

One of the most critical elements in the landscaping of rock and alpine gardens is the composition of the soil. Good drainage is the most important soil requirement, yet your soil must still be capable of retaining moisture sufficiently for the plants to grow successfully. Now, it may seem that the terms "well-drained" and "moisture-retentive" are at odds, but in fact you can build up your soil so that it has both of these qualities.

Examine the existing soil in your garden to determine if it is heavy clay or chalk; of a medium, loamy texture, or light and sandy. This can easily be done by taking a small handful of soil, and adding a little water. The aim is to roll the soil into a "thread", a sausage-shaped cylinder. The way in which this thread responds to handling will determine the soil texture:

• Heavy, clay soil will form a smooth thread that is easy to bend without splitting.

• Light, sandy soil will form a crumbly thread that will fall apart when bent.

• Loamy soil will form a solid thread that is slightly crumbly when bent.

Both the heavy and the light soil will need to be adjusted to perform well in a rockery. Be prepared, if the soil is very heavy and badly drained, to replace it entirely with imported topsoil that has been mixed with well-aged manure and compost. If the soil is only moderately heavy, it can be made more friable with the addition of any good organic matter (compost, peat, well-aged manures) and some coarse river sand. Very light soils can improve by adding peat, leaf mould, and other organic matter (compost and well-aged manures).

Once you have prepared a good batch of all-purpose soil to fill in around the rocks, take special note of individual plant requirements, because you may need to vary the soil from one part of the rock garden to another according to these specific requirements. We have already seen that most alpine species prefer an alkaline soil. If the existing soil is slightly acidic, add dolomite lime to sweeten it. Other species may prefer an acid soil, and this can be provided in the particular pockets of soil where they are to be grown.

Different plants may also require different types of soil. True alpines are best grown in shale, scree, or gravel pockets, and again this can be created within the overall framework of your rock or alpine garden. Add a quantity of gravel or fine pebbles, as much as 50 percent of the volume of the soil, because this will allow the plants to send their long roots deep into every crevice, protecting them from both heat and cold.

In general, if you study the individual soil requirements of each plant, you will have a much greater chance of success.

PREPARING FOR CONSTRUCTION

When you are building a rockery, the time you spend preparing the site, arranging the rocks and increasing the fertility of the soil will help ensure that the garden will flourish. The ground beneath the rocks must be free draining, and completely cleared of weed or lawn growth, which can cause a great deal of damage to the finished garden.

DRAINAGE

First check the ground to ensure it has good drainage. As we have seen, a heavy clay base will trap water, and the result will be that the pockets of soil will be too moist for the successful growing of these particular plants. Dig a hole to a depth of 2ft (60cm) and fill it with water from your garden hose. Allow an hour for the water to drain away completely from the hole.

If water remains after an hour, this is a good indication that certain steps will be needed to improve the drainage situation.

In the worst case, underground drainage pipes may need to be installed, to carry water away from the base of the garden. A more simple solution is to add a thick layer, at least 6in (15cm), of sand or a very light, sandy loam, as a base upon which the rockery can then be built.

WEEDS

The next challenge is the eradication of weed and lawn from the site. Weedkillers and herbicides are not advisable, because many alpine and rockery plants are

ABOVE: *A variety of growing situations, from built-up beds to containers and sloping beds, will mean that a wide range of plants can be accommodated. The soil mix may need to vary from one situation to the next.*

sensitive to chemicals, and may perish if there are residuals left in the soil. The best advice is to remove as many weeds as possible with a hoe, and then smother the weeds with a very thick covering of newspaper. Plastic sheeting has sometimes been used in the past, but this will never break down and can cause further problems with drainage. Instead, save all those old newspapers, and place them over the soil surface in a layer of at least 20 pages.

If it is necessary to correct the ground-level drainage with a sand or soil layer, this should be added on top of the newspaper layer. Eventually the papers will break down, but by that time the roots of any weeds or lawn will have been completely destroyed.

BUILDING YOUR GARDEN

If your rock garden is located on a sloping site, start the building process at the base of the slope, and then work upward. As each layer is set in place, pack the soil mixture firmly around the rocks, and, for stability, ensure that about half the volume of each rock is below soil level.

POSITIONING ROCK AND STONE

The same principle applies when positioning medium and smaller rocks between a framework of large boulders. As each layer is completed, walk on the stones to ensure they are firmly bedded in place. It is important that the stones carry your weight without shifting, as you will be clambering over them when planting and maintaining your rock garden.

The most back-breaking task, when you are constructing your rockery, is having to move the rock and stone. To avoid serious back injury, try to have assistance when lifting heavy pieces of rock. It is also a good idea to wear thick gloves and solid shoes when handling rock. A sturdy trolley, like those used to move boxes in the supermarket, is a useful device for shifting

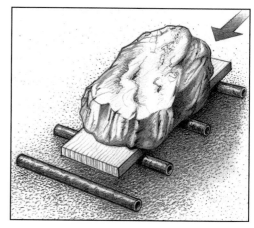

Fig. 1:
Large boulders can be moved from one area to another on rollers, providing the ground is relatively level, and there are no obstacles.

medium-sized and smaller rocks. Large boulders or heavy lumps of stone can be moved by using rollers (Fig. 1), or the age-old lever method (Fig. 2). Where really huge rocks are being included in the design, a small earthmoving vehicle or crane may be required, to lift each piece into place.

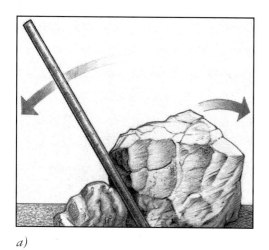

a)

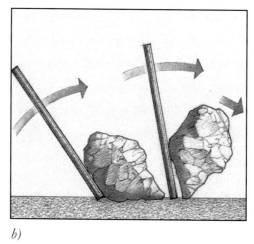

b)

c)

Fig. 2:
a) A lever can be used to shift large rocks, with a smaller stone being used as the fulcrum.
b) A lever can also be used to turn a boulder over, however never on a slope where it may start a landslide.
c) Various trolley designs that can be used for taking the back-breaking effort out of moving rocks.

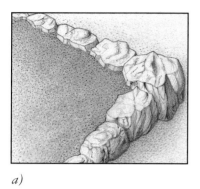

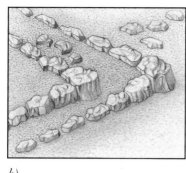

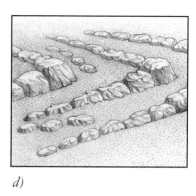

a)　　　　　　　　　　*b)*　　　　　　　　　　*c)*　　　　　　　　　　*d)*

Fig. 3: Building a Rock Garden Step-by-step

a) Create a rocky outcrop by starting at ground level, using a variety of sizes, with the largest on the corner and then decreasing in size towards the edges.

b) Backfill behind the first row of rocks with some free-draining soil mix, then add a second row following the same basic outline.

c) The third row can be positioned slightly higher up the slope, again using the largest rock for the cornerstone.

d) This pattern can be repeated according to the size of the garden. Backfill between each row with well drained, but moisture-retentive soil mix.

Use the largest rocks to form the framework of the garden, and once they are in place the smaller rocks can be positioned. Spread the medium and small rocks out around the edge of the garden, and then turn each one over to see the most attractive surface. Be prepared to spend some time doing this, to ensure that you will achieve the best effect.

Where possible, tilt rocks back in the same direction as the slope (Fig. 3), so that water runs into the garden soil rather than cascading over the surface. Layer the rocks so that they overlap, like bricks in a wall, rather than sitting one on top of the other. This will help to hold the soil pockets in together, and prevent the formation of channels that will wash the soil away when it rains. When the plants are established, their roots will help bind the entire structure together. In the meantime, however, place rocks in a way that will prevent any soil wash-away.

In some situations, the plants are incorporated into the rockery during the building process. Refer to Chapter Four for more information.

ABOVE: A pathway through a sloping rockery has been made using flat-topped concrete stepping stones. Paths are a good idea in larger rockeries, to provide easy access for general maintenance.

PLANTING & MAINTENANCE

The pleasure of planting

There are two basic ways of planting out a rockery garden. Some gardeners prefer to "plant as they go", incorporating their alpine and rockery specimens into the soil pockets during the actual construction process. Others wait until the structure of the rock garden has been completed, and then decide the best position for each plant according to size, colour, foliage, and growth habit. In this situation, it is easier to visualize the finished effect and to combine plants thoughtfully.

However, "planting as you go" has several advantages. It will allow you to ensure the plants are well bedded in place, and will probably help them to become established with less trauma. Crevice plants, in particular, benefit from this treatment.

OPPOSITE: Plants will thrive if rich pockets of soil are created between the rocks. Crevice plants can be incorporated during construction, and larger species planted when the basic structure is complete.

PREVIOUS PAGE: The extraordinary silvery foliage of Convolvulus boissieri *is covered with fine hairs, while the pale shell pink flowers that dot the plant, appear in late spring or early summer.*

There is always a risk that plants will be damaged during all the clambering around that is inevitable during the construction process. Another problem is that, once the rockery is completed, you may decide on different positions for plants already in place. However, if you have prepared a reasonably detailed ground plan, and are confident that the shape of the structure is not about to change, do place plants in their final positions while setting the rocks in place.

It is always best to avoid the hottest time of the day for planting; early mornings or evenings are the ideal time for this pleasurable task. Plants should be kept in a shady position, and watered well the day before they are transplanted into the garden. Water the rockery well the day before too, as transplanting into dry soil can be disastrous for the more sensitive species. Watering also helps the rocks and soil to settle into place.

Before you begin to plant, place the plants, still in their pots, in the rock garden in what you think will be their final positions, and then stand back and assess the effect. Also try to position the sun-loving varieties in spots that will get maximum sun, and the shade-lovers in pockets behind larger rocks, where they will get some protection from the sun. Try to achieve a balanced distribution of flower hues, and foliage textures and shades, so that the finished garden will look harmonious. You may also need to vary the soil and drainage material from one pocket to the next, according to the particular requirements of each plant. For example, extra grit or gravel can be added to those that like really arid soil conditions.

When you are ready to transplant, carefully remove the plants from their pots and gently compress the rootball into the shape of the pocket or crevice where it is to be planted. It is important that the roots are in contact with the soil mixture and not bare rock, if they are to spread and settle into place. Insert the roots firmly into the soil pocket, and press down well. If possible, label the plants when they are in position, so that you will become familiar with the location of each species or cultivar. Water well, and keep watering consistently until the plants become established, remembering that the rock may take up moisture from the soil, and that this moisture will then dry up in hot weather.

MAINTAINING THE GARDEN

The rockery or alpine garden needs care, as does the rest of your garden. Watering, weeding, feeding, and pest management are particularly important factors for the success of your rock garden.

ABOVE: Although rockery plants cannot withstand wet root conditions, they must still be watered frequently in hot, drying weather.

RIGHT: Gaps between plants should be mulched to prevent the soil pockets from drying out, and this can be done with a good layer of organic matter, providing it is not taken too close to the stems of the plants.

WATERING

In spite of the fact that most alpine and rockery plants like well-drained soil conditions, this does not mean that they can survive without being watered. Indeed, many varieties will be lost if the garden is left to its own devices. Factors to consider when working out a watering regime include the position of the garden (it will generally be in full sun), the weather in summer and winter, the amount of natural rainfall, and the soil type. Water supply is a priority if you want to achieve the best possible growing conditions.

Watering requirements will vary greatly according to the climate of the area in which the garden is located. Where hot, dry summers are experienced, watering weekly — sometimes even more frequently — is essential. As with all parts of the garden, deep watering of the rock garden is much more effective, because it encourages the plant's roots to travel downward in search of moisture. This is particularly true of alpines, which have a long root run and need the water to reach the root ends. Shallow watering will reverse the situation, with the plant's roots rising to find the water; thus the plant will be weakened.

In summer, water in the evening, as this will maximize the moisture loss

ABOVE: A thick gravel mulch is ideal because it prevents weed growth around plants, and blends in well with the rocky surroundings. Gravel does not create high humidity at ground level, which is good for many alpine species.

MULCHING

One of the most effective ways of keeping any garden healthy is mulching the soil surface. Mulching has several major benefits; for example, it suppresses weeds, and prevents the soil from drying out in hot or windy weather.

While most areas of the garden prefer an organic mulch, such as a well-aged manure, compost, or pine bark, this can cause problems in the rockery or alpine garden. When mulch layers are brought too close to the stems of sensitive plants, the humidity levels immediately around the base of the plant are increased, and this in turn can cause fungal problems. Therefore a mulch layer of gravel, blue metal screenings, or other rocky material will be far more satisfactory because it will allow the air to circulate freely around the plants while still keeping those weeds at bay. The main disadvantage of this type of mulch is that it will not supply nutrients to plants. However, if you follow the advice given in "Feeding and soil renewal" below, this problem can be overcome.

WEEDING

The weed is the natural enemy of the rock garden, and if allowed to take a stranglehold will be impossible to eradicate successfully. Prevention is better than cure, so ensure that the site is completely free of weeds and grass before the main structure of the rockery is built (also see Chapter Three). Mulching around each plant with a good thick layer of gravel or blue metal will also help to keep weed growth down, especially annual weeds that spring up from seed.

Remove any new weeds immediately they appear. Insert a knife into the soil

that occurs during the day. However, in exceptionally hot weather, especially if hot winds are blowing, water any time the garden appears stressed. Over-watering in winter is not recommended, and regular checks should be made to ensure the soil is no more than lightly moist. Too much water, in combination with

very cold temperatures or icy winds, can be the death knell for certain plants.

Learn to be a good observer, checking the garden frequently to judge when it needs water. By doing this, you will develop a watering regime that is suited to the requirements of your entire garden.

beside the weed to loosen the grip of the roots, and then lift them out carefully, to ensure the entire root is removed. In a recently constructed garden, weed remnants may be present in the soil mix, and these will be responsible for most of the weed growth that appears in the first few months. Keep on top of the problem by removing weeds on sight. Weeds may also be present in the soil of new plants that are introduced to the garden. Always check the potting soil thoroughly before transplanting, looking in particular for runners of couch grass that may be lurking there, because it will cause irrevocable damage if it takes off in the garden.

If they are neglected for several months, weeds will send their roots beneath and around rocks, making them very difficult to remove. The secret is to check routinely every week or so.

ABOVE: Check regularly for any sign of weed infestation, taking special care to eradicate any perennial weeds that may lodge between, and underneath, rocks. Remove annual weeds when they first seed.

LEFT: As the plants mature and spread to cover the soil surface between the rocks, the risk of weeds is greatly reduced. Renew organic mulch layers annually, to feed plants as well as to keep weed growth down.

FEEDING AND SOIL RENEWAL

In their natural environments, most alpine and rockery plants exist in soil that is not overly rich in nutrients. This is why the issue of feeding them is quite controversial. Overfeeding, especially with fertilizer that is high in nitrogen content, will cause lush growth of foliage at the expense of flowers.

In rock gardens and raised beds, where plants stay in the same soil all year round, the soil will become very thin and depleted as the nutrients are leached out after rain or watering. One way of supplying fresh nutrients to the soil is to add some freshly prepared soil mixture every year, preferably at the end of winter, when plant growth is dormant. This is done by carefully scraping away the mulch layer and putting it to one side, then filling in and around the plant with a rich mixture of peat, topsoil, and well-aged compost. On no account add manures or any organic matter that has not been well aged, as this will burn the sensitive roots of the plants.

If fertilizer is necessary, this should be applied at the same time as the topsoil is renewed. Never use powerful, fast-acting fertilizers, as many of the species in the garden will resent this sudden burst of nutrients. Instead, use a slow-release organic fertilizer in powdered or granular form. Ensure that it has an equal balance of nitrogen, phosphorus, and potassium for the best results.

RIGHT: Potted plants are entirely dependent on the gardener for nutrients, and they should be fed a slow-release organic fertilizer, applied at the beginning of the main growing period in spring.

ABOVE: It is essential to grow many species under glass in cool to cold climates where winter rain and frost can cause damage. Ensure good air ventilation through the glasshouse, as high humidity can cause fungal problems.

WINTER PROTECTION

Most alpine plants are quite hardy, and do not suffer from the cold temperatures experienced in winter. However, icy winds and frosts can be a major problem for those species that are more sensitive. True alpines, found wild above the tree line, are covered with snow during winter, and this is like a blanket that protects them from the wind and from harsh frosts. Without this covering they are vulnerable, especially if a period of warm weather is experienced, followed by a sudden cold snap. The warmth will have encouraged tender new growth, and the sudden drop in temperature can cause tremendous damage.

In cool to cold climates these sensitive plants will need to be lifted in winter and kept in an alpine house for protection. They can also be protected by small hessian screens that will keep off the frost and reduce the impact of icy winds. For protection on a larger scale a lean-to can be erected in winter to shelter the entire alpine garden, but this is probably only necessary when true alpines are being grown.

Try to select only those species of rockery or alpine plant that are known to do well in your particular climate conditions, and if possible position plants that need protection behind a large rock or in a warm pocket, where they will not experience too many difficulties. Avoid over-watering in winter, and check regularly to see how the garden is weathering the cold.

PEST AND DISEASE MANAGEMENT

Alpine and rockery plants are no more, or less, susceptible to insect attack or disease infestation than are any other garden plants. There are several basic but extremely useful ground rules for prevention of problems.

In particular, it is important, when growing plants outside, to select species capable of surviving in the climate of the area where they are to be grown. While it can be said that all "true" alpines are being grown away from their natural environment, this should not prove problematic if the correct growing conditions (suitable soil, watering, and shelter) are provided. However, when plants have to struggle to survive, competing with weeds or suffering in an alien climate, they will naturally be much more susceptible to pests and diseases. Therefore, always choose plants that are hardy enough to tough it out.

The second factor affecting the resistance of plants to pest attacks and disease is the conditions in which they are grown. This was briefly touched on above. If the garden bed has been well prepared, with adequate drainage, and a good, healthy soil mixture, the plants will be more robust, and again this means they will be less vulnerable to common problems.

Hygiene is important, too. If dead vegetation and weeds are left lying around, they will provide a breeding place for insects. When deadheading plants, don't just throw the spent flowers on the ground. Instead, add them to a compost pile that is well away from the garden. Any new plants that are introduced, especially in the enclosed conditions of a glasshouse, should also be checked thoroughly for signs of ill health. They may be carrying insects or diseases that can be passed onto other plants in the collection. Introduce only healthy, disease-free plants and get them established quickly, before they have a chance to deteriorate.

Finally, keep a constant check on plants, especially by examining the backs of the leaves, to detect any indication of a problem. This is essential if problems are to be picked up and treated immediately, before they have an opportunity either to damage the plants severely, or spread to other plants. It might be a good idea to water the garden by hand, checking the plants as you go. This can be quite pleasurable, as it helps you to keep in close contact with your garden. Certain insects, such as snails, slugs and aphids, can be removed manually if they are only present in small numbers.

Despite all such precautions, you may still have problems with pests or disease. Avoid using chemicals, if possible, as so many of these plants are sensitive and may react badly to chemical contact.

PESTS

Snails, slugs and aphids are by far the most common problems in the rockery or alpine garden. Snails and slugs will attack young plants, while aphids will feed on tender new growth, including flower buds.

Try to keep snails and slugs under control by systematically removing them before they have a chance to build up in numbers. A saucer of beer in the garden will attract and kill them. Otherwise, try placing a timber plank across the ground. This will provide a place for them to hide, and then it is simply a matter of turning the plank over and removing them. Early evening, or periods just after rain, are good times to find snails and slugs out and about, and dispose of them. Some gardeners even go out at night with a torch and catch them in the act. However, if using snail baits, remember that they are extremely toxic to children and small animals, so use them sparingly and never sprinkle them so they land in a pile.

Aphids are common pests that can cause damage very quickly, so keep an eye out for them, especially in spring. If there are birds or ladybirds in the garden, they

ABOVE: Keep the area around plants free from weeds, and do not allow spent flowerheads or discarded prunings to lie around, especially if they are carrying disease.

will help control aphids biologically, which is preferable to spraying. Aphids can also be squashed and brushed off plants, but this will need to be done every day until the problem has passed. There is also a variety of relatively harmless pyrethrum-based "organic" garden sprays that can be useful in the event of a more widespread attack.

Caterpillars are leaf-eating pests that will trouble certain plants, but once again if caught early they should not be a problem. Check the backs of leaves and remove them manually.

Red spider mites can be a real problem in the glasshouse during hot, dry weather. The mites are too small to be seen with the naked eye, and they attack foliage and cause mottling and eventually withering. If plants are not doing well then examine the backs of the foliage for any sign of red mottling or webbing, as this is a good indication that mites are present. Red spider mites have developed a resistance to spraying, so investigate biological control methods, which involve releasing predatory mites that will feast on the red spider mites that are causing all the damage. The predatory mites will die when they have eliminated the pests, and not cause any more damage.

DISEASES

Fungal diseases are probably the only ones that will be a problem to rockery or alpine plants. These are caused either when the soil becomes waterlogged, or when the humidity at ground level is too great. If you are screening or covering plants to protect them from the cold or from heavy rainfall, this can trap

moisture and increase the humidity, which again will cause a problem. Also, if weeds are allowed to proliferate around plants, these will reduce air movement, as well as weakening plants, because they will be forced to compete for moisture and nutrients.

There are several ways of preventing fungal disease. Keep the garden or containers weed-free and well ventilated. Instead of using a thick organic mulch, use gravel or stone chips to keep weeds down. If you use mulch, keep mulch

layers away from the stems of plants, to let the air circulate. Make sure the soil is well drained, and be careful not to overwater, especially during winter. When plants are grown in a glasshouse, cross-ventilation is very important, as this will keep the air moving freely around the plants, and prevent fungus or rot.

These simple measures should be sufficient to ensure that the plants in your rock and alpine gardens remain healthy and disease-free.

ABOVE: Select robust species, such as sedum and geranium, which are not generally troubled by pest or disease problems.

PROPAGATION

Basic techniques

Learning basic propagation techniques is a way of gaining further understanding about the entire subject of horticulture. Those gardeners who become interested in all the fascinating aspects of plant cultivation usually progress to the point of wanting to learn how to produce their own plants from their own gardens. Propagating plants is very satisfying, and obviously has the advantage of saving money as well. The joy is that propagation is really not all that difficult, once a few standard ground rules are understood.

Different plants are propagated in different ways, according to their structure and growth pattern, although there are many plants that can be reproduced using more than one method of propagation. Collecting seed, taking cuttings, and division are the easiest and most commonly used and successful methods of home propagation, especially for alpine and rockery plants.

COLLECTING AND SOWING SEEDS

In the wild, true flowering plants increase and spread by dropping seed every year, which scatters to the wind and self-sows in the ground. In the garden this natural process can be assisted by gathering the seed of annual garden plants in autumn, and either sowing it directly in the ground where it is to grow, or storing the seed and sowing it the following spring.

If gathering your own seed from the garden, keep in mind that only non-hybridized plants will reproduce true to type. So it helps to know which of your plants are species, and will give you viable seeds for propagation.

The process of seed gathering begins when the spent flower heads begin to turn brown and dry out, which is generally at the end of the main flowering season in autumn, although early spring-flowering plants will be ready to have their seeds harvested much earlier. Check the plants daily, and when the seed heads are dry, shake the seeds gently into a paper bag. Alternatively, tie paper bags over the seed heads for a few days, so that the seeds will naturally drop off when the heads are completely dry. This process, however, can be spoilt if sudden rain dampens the paper bag and seeds!

OPPOSITE: Sempervivums are extremely easy to propagate, simply by cutting off individual rosettes with a sharp knife, and planting them directly in the ground where they are to grow.

PREVIOUS PAGE: The spectacular yellow and white flowers of Limnanthes douglasii, *also known as butter and eggs, which can be invasive in small gardens.*

ABOVE: Alyssum saxatile *is quite easily propagated from cuttings, which can be taken from mid to late summer. It looks most effective when mass planted along the border or edge of the rockery.*

Germinating plants from seed, whether they are home harvested or commercial seed, involves providing a moist and sheltered growing environment. For the best results sow seeds in trays of specially formulated seed raising mixture, which provides the right texture and nutrients to get plants up and growing easily. More experienced gardeners often make their own mix, by adding extra grit and peat to a commercial potting mix. Once sown the soil must be kept lightly moist, never wet, until germination, which varies greatly according to the species. Annuals usually germinate quite rapidly, in ten days to three weeks; however, many alpine plants may take much longer, and in fact may not germinate until the following season. The seed trays should be kept in a shady, protected place and then transplanted into larger containers when the seedlings have reached 4in (10cm) in height.

When planted out in the garden, young seedlings will need to be protected from snails and slugs, and watered well until they become established.

ABOVE: The seed of Ranunculus calandriniodes *can be collected when the flowerheads become dry, but must be sown immediately in a moist, well-drained seed-raising mixture.*

DIVISION

This is the easiest way of propagating most perennials, as well as a great many alpines and other rockery plants that are tufted or clump-forming. Division basically refers to the process of dividing the plant into two or more clumps, or portions, that can then be transplanted wherever you want them in the garden.

To divide plants you must first ensure that the soil surrounding the plant is lightly damp — never dry and certainly never wet or waterlogged. Watering the plant thoroughly the day prior to lifting will create the right conditions. Spring and autumn are good seasons for this task, which should be done in the early morning or evening so that the exposed plant roots do not dry out. Use a spade to excavate a wide area around the plant roots, aiming to lift as much of the intact root mass as possible. When the plant has been lifted, attempt to separate it gently into portions, according to how many plants you wish to create from the main clump. The roots of herbaceous perennials are sometimes very tightly tangled, and you may need to dip the the whole root ball into a bucket of water to remove the soil, then tease the roots apart to separate them. Very large and difficult clumps may need to be separated by using two forks, back to back, which are then levered apart to separate the roots. Where plants have individual crowns, such as primulas and irises, but the roots are still strongly attached to each other, it may be necessary to sever them with a sharp knife or scalpel.

It is a good idea to plant out the clumps immediately, into ground that has been well prepared and is also lightly damp. If dividing plants in autumn you may wish to pot up the new clumps, and store them in a sheltered position until spring.

CUTTINGS

This is a slightly more technical form of propagating plants. However, it is highly successful if a few basic steps are followed. Most cuttings are taken in late summer while the plants are still experiencing active growth, although basal, or "heel" cuttings as they are sometimes known, are generally taken in spring.

The basic idea of taking cuttings is to remove a shoot from the parent plant and insert it into a growing medium that will encourage new root growth. Shoots taken for cuttings should never include any flowering material such as buds or flowers. As the roots grow, new leaf growth appears on the stem, and thus a new plant is formed.

Basal cuttings: most rock and alpine plants can be produced from this type of cutting. Examine the plant for shoots that arise at ground level, or just above ground level. Carefully remove the shoot by pulling downwards and outwards, so that a fine strip or "heel" of tissue is attached to the shoot. At the top of the stem all but about five or six leaves should be removed, and then the base of the cutting dipped in a rooting hormone before being potted up. Do not allow the potting mixture to dry out, but also take care not to overwater. When new top growth appears it indicates that roots have formed, and after several weeks the plant will be ready to plant into the garden.

Tip cuttings: these are also called nodal cuttings. Simply cut a section of stem beneath a leaf or leaf pair, and trim some of the leaves from the top so that the finished cutting measures no more than 3/4in (3cm) in length. With small cushion-forming plants the length of the cutting will obviously be far smaller. Again dip the cut tip into a rooting hormone before inserting into the growing medium.

Leaf cuttings: a few rockery plants can be propagated by removing an outside leaf from the plant in spring, cutting it as close to main stem as possible using a clean, sharp knife. The leaf is then inserted into a mixture of sharp sand and peat (1 part of each), to a depth of 1/2in (1.25cm). The pot should be placed in a shaded, sheltered position and kept lightly moist until roots form. *Sedum* sp. and *Ramonda* sp. are plants that can be propagated this way.

ABOVE: Crepis aurea *is an annual for the rockery that is propagated by seed. It can be invasive in small gardens.*

RIGHT: Pretty pink dianthus are easily propagated from seed, while campanula is generally propagated by division of the clumps in early spring.

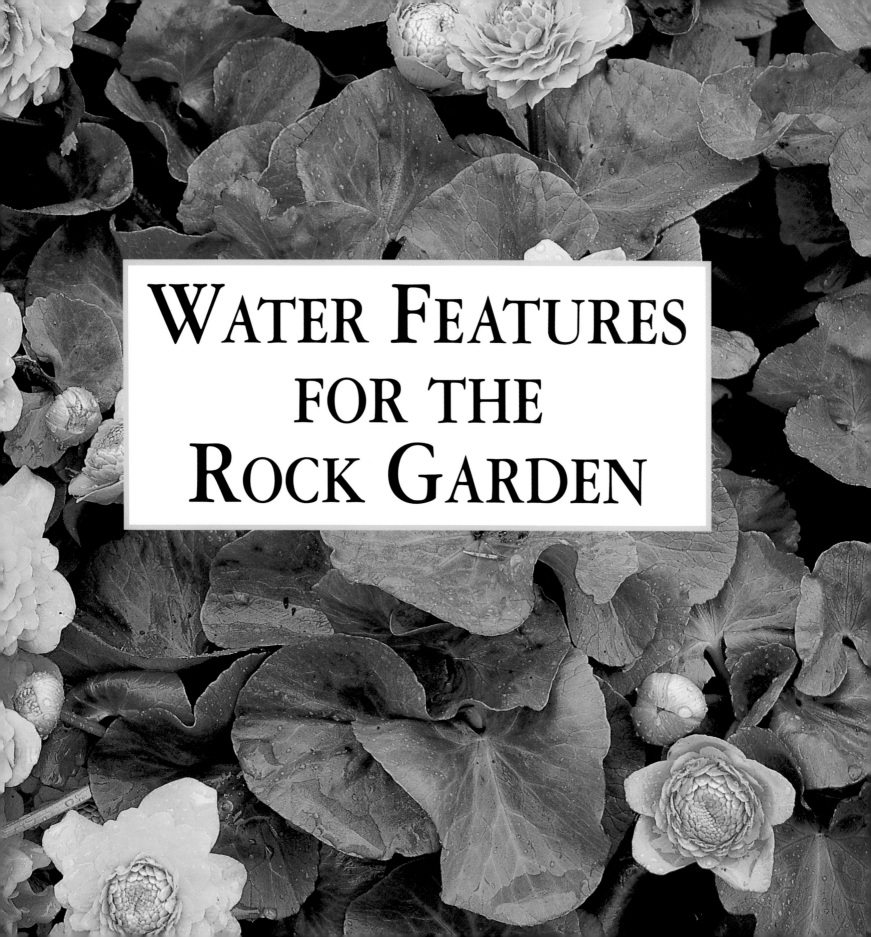

WATER FEATURES
FOR THE
ROCK GARDEN

Water and plants in harmony

While water is never used as a feature in traditional alpine gardens, it is a popular and simple way of adding interest and texture to a rock garden. Indeed, rocks and water are perfect companions, and this style of garden is often seen in warmer climates, where there is scope for a wide range of interesting plants that combine well with water features.

There are many forms in which water can be integrated into a rock garden — from a small pool to an elaborate waterfall, a cascade or a stream. The sight and sound of moving water always adds an extra element of excitement to the garden, and in the context of a rock garden it is especially appealing.

Unless you are planning a stylized contemporary garden, try to keep the water features looking as natural as possible. The way in which the rocks are

OPPOSITE: A simple water feature, like this trough of stones that shine when splashed by water from a single-stream fountain, will bring movement and light to the garden.

PREVIOUS PAGE: The vigorous Caltha palustris, *or common marsh marigold, thrives in the damp, boggy soil conditions at the edge of streams or ponds.*

placed will have a great deal to do with this effect. Examine each rock carefully before setting it in position, turning it over to reveal the most interesting "face". Never place rocks at odd angles or on their sides, as this will detract from the "natural" look. Around the edges of ponds and down the sides of waterfalls, the rocks should be allowed to overhang, to hide any sight of the concrete or rubber lining of the structures. Plants should then be tucked in between the rocks, with those with a trailing habit placed near the edges to add a softening touch, and to catch the reflection of the water.

The only potential problem with a garden that combines rockery plants and water is poor drainage. Ensure that the drainage around the water garden is excellent at all times, and that the ground-level humidity does not increase, causing fungal problems for the more sensitive species.

A great deal will depend on how the garden is designed and built. The same basic principles apply as those for the construction of a rock garden. Therefore, be constantly aware of the need for good drainage in the soil beneath the rockery as a whole, as well as in the individual pockets between rocks where the plants are to grow. Water features are

often positioned at low points in the garden. If the ground there is boggy or otherwise unsuitable for cultivation, additional precautions need to be taken when placing the rocks around the edge of the lake or pool, so that the correct growing conditions are still provided.

WATERFALLS AND CASCADES

Moving water from one level of the garden to another is a delightful way of creating a feeling of spaciousness in the garden. Waterfalls are usually built on ground that slopes naturally, although sometimes the levels need to be created artificially, and built up with large boulders to give the back of the waterfall the necessary height. Take care, if removing topsoil during excavation, that it does not affect the subsoil and subsequently make drainage more difficult. Small pumps will be required to take the water from the base to the top of the waterfall, and the constant movement of water will ensure that the water is clean and clear, with a good oxygen supply for any fish or plants that may be added. Keep the water flow to a gentle trickle rather than a gushing torrent, because this will prevent water from splashing over the edges and affecting nearby plants that may resent damp conditions.

ABOVE: *For this dramatic waterfall large feature stones have been placed at angles and on their sides to give the height required. The water is recirculated using a small submersible pump.*

OPPOSITE: *Around the ponds and waterfalls, pockets of soil with excellent drainage allow for rockery plants to be grown without being affected by the increased moisture.*

OPPOSITE: *The effective use of conifers to frame a cascading waterfall. Plants located near the edge of the water need to be species that can cope with the increase in soil and air moisture.*

PONDS AND POOLS

The most popular and also the easiest way of bringing water into the garden is to make a small garden pool that is surrounded by natural rocky outcrops. There are various types, including concrete and rubber-lined pools, and the choice will depend on your budget and building expertise. Rubber-lined pools are the easiest to construct, and the more recently developed lining materials are strong enough to last for decades, unless they get punctured.

Unless the pond has a fountain, the water will be still and therefore in danger of becoming stagnant. The addition of oxygenating plants and fish will help to counteract this problem, although it may still be necessary to flush the pond with clean water during hot weather, when there is a danger of sudden algal growth. Keep the water clear of fallen leaves and organic debris, which will break down and add to the problem of dirty water.

STREAMS

A small stream or brook running through the bottom of a garden is a feature that most of us admire. If the surrounds are sunny and open, there is scope for building a rock garden along the stream banks, and filling it with plants that will cascade over the edges. Ensure that the drainage is good and prepare the site well to avoid weed or grass infestation. If the water flow is not too fast, there will be scope for marginal and deep water plantings that will complement the rockery plants used along the edges. Fast-flowing water will dislodge plants and wash them downstream, unless a dam wall is built to slow the movement of the water.

ABOVE: Smooth river stones surround a small water garden that is the central feature of a scree for growing a variety of rockery plants.

PLANTING
GUIDE

Plants for rock and alpine gardens

Acaena microphylla
New Zealand burr

A native of New Zealand that resembles wild strawberry, mat-forming, with silver-grey foliage that turns bronze with age. Has bright red burrs in summer. Can be grown as an alpine lawn.

Achillea aurea
Yarrow

A spectacular perennial with bright green foliage, and tiny golden flowers borne on stems that grow up to 9in (23cm) long. Requires full sun \and is easy to grow. Has a lengthy flowering period.

Aconitum napellus
Monkshood

A tuft-forming perennial with delicate, divided foliage and dense racemes of blooms in a deep purple. Will grow to

OPPOSITE: Alyssum montanum
(mountain alyssum)

PREVIOUS PAGE: Iberis semperflorens
(candytuft)

about 2ft 8in (80cm), and is easy to cultivate in partially shaded areas. Extremely poisonous.

Adonis vernalis

An attractive herbaceous perennial, forming clumps of rich green foliage and large golden flowers, produced in spring. May reach 16in (40cm) in height if cultivated in an open, sunny position. Good plant for beginners.

Aethionema grandiflorum

Has blue-green foliage and stems forming tufts up to 12in (30cm) tall. Requires full sun and is easiest to cultivate in a well-drained, gritty soil. Has rose-pink flowers in spring and summer, and a trailing habit.

Ajuga reptans
Bugle flower

A vigorous perennial that forms a carpet-like mat of foliage. Has shiny green or deep bronze leaves, inter-spersed with spikes of blue, pink, or white flowers. Will thrive in full sun or partial shade, and is quite easy to grow in moist soil.

Alchemilla alpina
Lady's mantle

This perennial forms low tufts of delightful green foliage with striking silvery undersides. Produces masses of tiny yellow-green blooms in summer. Easy to cultivate, and will thrive in a semi-shaded position.

Alchemilla mollis
Lady's mantle

A clump-forming perennial with delicate grey-green foliage. Clusters of green-yellow flowers appear in summer, with a sprawling habit suitable for paving or at water's edge. Easy to grow in sun or semi-shade.

Alyssum sp.
Sweet Alice

A popular group of annuals and perennials, usually forming mats or tufts of foliage with clusters of yellow, pink, or white flowers. Easy to cultivate in an open and sunny position. Seeds can be sown between pavers or in crevices. Good plant for beginners.

ABOVE: Androsace sarmentosa *(rock jasmine)*

Androsace sp.

A large and useful genus of rockery and alpine plants that vary greatly in their appearance. Many form a cushion of leafy rosettes studded with single flowers or stalked umbels. In general require a well-drained and moist soil, and should be planted in a sunny position. Easy to cultivate, ideal for scree beds or between paving stones.

Anemone nemorosa
Wood anemone

A delightful small plant with whorls of toothed leaves, and flowers in a variety of shades, including lavender-blue and white. Thrives in a sunny or semi-shaded position, and is easy to grow.

Anemonella thalictroides

Forms tufts of slender stems with finely divided foliage. Grows to 12cm (5in) in height. Produces tiny white or pale pink flowers in spring. Best results in shady and sheltered positions. Easy to cultivate.

Anaphalis nubigenus

Forms tufts of long stems and silver-grey foliage. Flower heads are yellow-white — the male blooms are tubular in aspect, while the female blooms are slim and thread-like. Requires full sun and well-drained soil.

Anchusa caespitosa

A tiny alpine species with dark green foliage. Has clusters of gentian blue flowers in spring. Requires an open sunny position and well-drained, gritty soil. Difficult to grow, not recommended for the beginner.

Andromeda polifiolia

A dwarf evergreen shrub forming a hummock up to 18in (45cm) tall. Has deep green foliage and a spreading shape. White or pale pink flowers are produced in summer. Requires full sun or partial shade, and an acid soil.

Anthemis nobilis
Chamomile

This popular group of plants is ideal for alpine lawns and rock gardens, with bright green, aromatic foliage and heads of delicate white blooms, yellow in the centre. Thrives in a sunny position and is easy to cultivate.

ABOVE: Aquilegia alpina *(alpine columbine)*

ABOVE: Adonis vernalis

Anthirrhinum molle
Soft snapdragon

This perennial has a trailing habit, and stems covered in soft mid-green foliage. The flowers, which bloom in summer, are generally white, flushed with golden-yellow. Plant in a shady, sheltered position. Also ideal for crevice plantings.

Anthyllis vulneraria
Kidney vetch

A biennial or perennial that can reach 12in (30cm) in height. Flowers appear in late spring and summer, generally yellow, and turn orange with age. Easy-care plant for a sunny position.

Aquilegia alpina
Alpine columbine

A charming plant, growing to 2ft (60cm) in height, with grey-green foliage and spurs of large blue flowers in summer. Easy to grow in a sunny spot. However, difficult to maintain as it crosses readily with other cultivars.

Much taller than most plants grown in an alpine garden, but great for the back of a rockery.

Arabis alpina
Alpine rockcress

Forms a low-spreading mat of leafy rosettes, with white or pale pink flowers borne above the foliage in spring and summer. Prefers a gravelly, moist soil, and either a sunny or partially shaded position. Easy to grow, a good plant for beginners.

ABOVE: Armeria maritima *(thrift)*

Armeria maritima
Thrift

This easy-to-cultivate plant grows in low clumps of deep green foliage, with flowers that range from white to a deep rose-pink in spring and summer. Prefers a sunny position and soil that has not been over-enriched.

Arnica montana
Alpine arnica

A rhizomatous perennial with rosettes of hairy foliage and tall stems that carry single golden-yellow blooms in late spring and early summer. Prefers full sun and an alkaline soil. Quite a fussy plant that does not enjoy being moved.

Artemisia pedemontana

A delightful herbaceous perennial with a neat shape and finely divided foliage. Both the leaves and yellow flowers are covered in fine white hairs. Grows from $1^{1}/_{2}$in (4cm) to $2^{1}/_{2}$in (6cm) in height and prefers full sun.

Arctostaphylos alpinus
Bear berry

This attractive plant forms a low carpet of silvery foliage on reddish trailing stems. White flowers, often flushed with pink or green, appear in spring and early summer. Also produces dark, succulent berries. Plant in full sun or partial shade, in slightly acid soil.

Arenaria purpurascens
Sandwort

Rosettes of leaves form a loose cushion of foliage. Clusters of light purple or white flowers are produced above this foliage in summer. Will thrive in full sun or partial shade, in a moist soil. Easy to grow, and is sometimes used as an alpine lawn.

Asperula suberosa
Woodruff

A popular alpine plant that forms a low tufted cushion of silvery leaves. Flower spikes produce clusters of tubular pink blooms in early summer. Prefers a sunny position and well-drained soil. Quite a sensitive plant, often only grown in an alpine house.

Aster alpinus
Alpine aster

A most attractive plant with rosettes of leaves covered with soft white hairs and masses of purple, pink, or white flowers in late spring and early summer. Easy to grow in a sunny position, a good plant for beginners.

Astilbe simplicifolia

Will reach 8in (20cm) in height and is characterized by delicate, fern-like foliage. Most cultivars produce white flower spikes in late summer. Plant in a shady and sheltered position, in well-drained but moist soil.

Astrantia minor

A branching, tufted perennial with lobed foliage and clusters of white flowers, which are circled by distinctive serrated bracts. Blooms are produced in summer. Grow in a sunny or partially shaded position.

Aubrieta deltoidea

Has numerous cultivars, all of which are easy to cultivate. Forms dense mats of grey-green leafy rosettes. Masses of flowers, usually in shades of purple or pink, are produced in spring. Prefers full sun.

Azorella trifurcata

A perennial forming low cushions of foliage that is leathery and a shiny apple-green. Small yellow flowers are

ABOVE: Aster alpinus *(alpine aster)*

borne close to the foliage in summer. Plant in partial shade.

Baeckia camphorosmae

A shrubby evergreen growing up to 2ft 4in (70cm) tall, with tiny aromatic leaves that cover its numerous branches. The flowers are white or pink and are produced in early summer. Prefers

partial sun and a warm position. Versatile and easy to grow.

Betula nana
Dwarf birch

A hardy, dwarf shrub growing to 1ft (30cm), with small leaves that turn yellow in fall (autumn) before falling. Very pleasant winter outline.

ABOVE: Campanula cochleariifolia *(bellflower)*

Calandrinia caepitosa

A rare fleshy plant forming low tufts of grey-green foliage, less than 2in (5cm) high. Leaves are studded with white or cream flowers in late spring and summer. Requires full sun and is quite a challenge to cultivate.

Calceolaria darwinii
Slipper-wort

A short-lived perennial with dark green toothed foliage. The sticky green leaves form a mat, while each unusual single yellow-brown flower features a bold white bar across its lower lip. Difficult to grow, requiring a shaded position in a rich, gritty, acid soil.

Callianthemum anemonoides

This tiny plant has delicate blue-green foliage and produces white flowers marked with orange during spring. Plant in a sunny position in deep, moist, but well-drained soil. Easy to cultivate.

Calluna vulgaris

An evergreen dwarf shrub with numerous popular cultivars. It rarely exceeds 2ft (60cm), and has delicate grey-green foliage and flower spikes producing dense clusters of pinkish purple blooms in summer. Prefers full sun and an acid soil.

Caltha palustris

In this genus the lower, spreading cultivars are suitable for rock gardens, and do best in moist soil. The leaves are large and shiny, while the glossy golden blooms are produced in spring. Easy to grow in full sun or partial shade.

Campanula carpatica
Bellflower

The most common species in cultivation, prized for its brilliant green foliage and wide, cup-like blooms. Flowers appear in late spring and vary in hue from purple to white. Prefers a sunny position. Easy to grow, can be planted in crevices or over dry walls.

Campanula cochleariifolia
Bellflower

Very easy to cultivate, this charming small plant forms mats of toothed, bright green foliage. Blue bell-like flowers are borne above the foliage on slender stems. Place in gritty soil in a sunny position. Rather rampant, can be invasive.

Campanula portenschlagiana
Bellflower

This perennial is a vigorous grower and forms tufts of branching stems covered in deep green foliage. The bell-like flowers are a delicate pale purple and appear in late summer. Easy to cultivate in sun or shade, an ideal plant for beginners.

Cardamine pratensis
Cuckoo flower/Lady's smock

Some cultivars, particularly 'Flore-pleno', are worthy of attention. It forms low clumps of mid-green foliage, covered with white or pink flowers in summer. Thrives in a semi-shaded, damp position.

Carlina acaulis
Stemless carlina thistle

This unusual plant is characterized by rosettes of large prickly leaves and creamy white flowers. It rarely exceeds a height of 3in (80mm). Easy to cultivate in a sunny position.

Cassiope fastigiata

A dwarf evergreen shrub, growing to a height of 12in (30cm), with scaly foliage and large white flowers in spring. Plant in partial shade in slightly acid soil.

Celmisia bellidioides

An easy-to-grow plant that forms a spreading carpet of glossy dark green

ABOVE: Clematis alpina

foliage, covered with masses of white daisy flowers in late spring and summer. Plant in partial shade in a moist, gravelly soil.

Centaurea montana

A vigorously spreading herbaceous plant that can be invasive, and is therefore suitable only for a large rock garden. Flower heads are surrounded by ornamental bracts, a rich pink or

purple. Plant in full sun or partial shade.

Cerastium alpinum
Alpine mouse-ear

A neat mat-forming plant with clumps of hair-covered foliage. Glossy white blooms are carried above the foliage in late spring and summer. Easy to cultivate, especially in a sunny position.

ABOVE: Convolvulus cneorum

Chamaecytisus purpureus (syn. *Cytisus purpureus*)

A small shrub reaching about 12in (30cm) in height, with attractive pink to purple blooms in late spring and summer. Prefers full sun.

Chamaepericlymenum canadense
Creeping dogwood

An interesting plant that forms a thick carpet of dark green foliage, and minute purple or violet flowers in late spring and summer, surrounded by ornamental bracts. Easy to cultivate, especially in partial shade in slightly acid soil.

Clematis alpina

A trailing or climbing plant with soft foliage and drooping blooms of a rich violet or powdery blue during summer. Not too invasive, ideal for clambering over rocky surfaces. Ensure roots are in the shade.

Codonopsis clematidea

The trailing stems of this scrambling twiner are covered with pale green leaves and bell-like pale blue flowers that bloom in summer. Will self-seed happily, prefers a sunny position.

Convolvulus boissieri

A woody-stemmed plant that forms a mat or low cushion up to 3in (8cm) in height, with interesting foliage that is silky, and a delicate silver shade. The pale pink flowers appear in summer. Plant in full sun and protect from winter wet.

Convolvulus cneorum

A compact shrubby bush reaching 20in (50cm) in height with hair-covered silver foliage and woolly buds that open to white flowers, flushed with pink in summer. Easy to grow, but tender. Plant in a sunny, sheltered position.

Coronilla minima

A useful perennial with grey-green foliage, growing to 4in (10cm) tall. The golden-yellow blooms have a sweet fragrance and are produced in clusters in late spring and summer. Easy to cultivate in a sunny, well-drained spot.

Corydalis lutea

A fibrous-rooted species, forming a mound of delicate green foliage. Masses of golden flower racemes are borne from spring to fall (autumn). Self-seeds easily in a sheltered position. Easy to grow.

Cotula striata

A fascinating plant that forms a carpet of hair-covered leaves in clusters on creeping stems. Striking clusters of reddish black flowers appear in late spring and early summer. Will thrive in sun or partial shade and is easy to cultivate, often planted in scree beds or between paving stones.

Crepis aurea
Hawkweed

A species with numerous variations in appearance. The leaves are either toothed or divided; some are hair-covered, others hairless. Flower stems also vary in length and carry orange-bronze flowers in summer. Rarely exceeds 3in (8cm) in height. Full sun.

Crocus sp.

A large genus of bulbs that pop up through the rocks, with the flowers preceding the foliage. Often grown in cool-climate rockeries. The flowers vary from pink and purple to yellow, according to the variety. Likes full sun and well-drained, moderately rich soil.

Cyclamen hederifolium

Growing to a height of 5in (12cm), this plant is prized for its variegated foliage, which is grey-green or silver. Solitary pale pink blooms are produced in late summer and fall (autumn). Easy to cultivate in a shady position.

ABOVE: Crocus species

Cyclamen mirabile

A dwarf species with delicately patterned, crimson-flushed foliage. Its pale pink flowers are produced in fall (autumn) and have distinctly toothed petals. Prefers a partially shaded position and is easy to grow.

Cytisus x praecox

A large shrub, reaching up to 9ft (3m) in height, although dwarf forms are available. Masses of cream flowers are borne in clusters during spring. Easy to grow. Prefers a sunny position.

Daphne alpina

An evergreen shrub that forms a loose clump of branches and grey-green foliage. Reaches 2ft 4in (70cm) in height, with creamy white flowers during spring and summer. Prefers full sun.

ABOVE: Dianthus alpinus *(dwarf pink)*

Daphne cneorum

An evergreen shrub with a trailing habit, with dark green foliage spreading up to 6¹/₂ft (2m) across. Fragrant pink flowers carried at the shoot tips in spring. Easy to cultivate in full sun.

Daphne mezereum

An erect branching shrub, usually growing to about 3ft (1m) in height. The pink or reddish purple fragrant flowers appear in clusters in early spring. Can be grown either in full sun or partial shade.

Delphinium muscosum

This delightful plant forms a low tuft of hair-covered foliage, studded with furry blue flowers in summer. Quite a fussy plant, requiring a well-drained soil and protection against slug attacks. Prefers a sunny position.

Dianthus alpinus
Dwarf pink

A cushion-forming perennial with widely spaced, narrow leaves and large solitary flowers of a purple-red shade, with paler spotting. Blooms in summer. Very easy to cultivate in a sunny position, ideal for the inexperienced gardener.

Dianthus deltoides
Dwarf pink

A mat-forming plant with wiry stems and narrow, spiked leaves. Grows up to 18in (45cm) tall, with pink or reddish flowers with a darker tint in the centre. Easily cultivated in a sunny position.

Dianthus glacialis
Dwarf pink

Similar to *Dianthus alpinus*, but much more compact, only reaching ³/₄in to 2in (2–5cm) in height. The flowers are a brilliant rose red and are produced on short stems during summer. Very easy to grow in full sun.

Dianthus petraeus
Dwarf pink

This charming plant forms an open, spiked cushion of greyish foliage. Fragrant solitary flowers, snowy white, are carried on stems above the leaves in summer. It is easy to grow in a sunny position.

Dicentra peregrina
Bleeding heart

Quite a rare plant, and difficult to grow, but well worth the effort with its tufts of silvery grey foliage and large clear pink blooms. Fern-like in appearance, with spurred flowers in late spring. Requires a sheltered position.

Dionysia aretioides

This plant features grey-green cushions of toothed leaves, studded with brilliant yellow flowers during spring. Most dionysias are temperamental. However, this one is easy to grow. Should thrive with good drainage and sunny position.

Draba aizoides

A cushion-forming perennial with bristly, deep green foliage and lemon-yellow flowers that bloom in spring. Quite a difficult plant to grow, and not recommended for beginners.

Dracocephalum grandiflorum

A native of Siberia, this perennial has a neat outline and heart-shaped leaves. Dense spikes of violet-blue flowers appear in late summer. Easily cultivated in a sunny position.

Dryas drummondii
Mountain aven

A small carpeting shrub with dark green foliage and a vigorous growing habit. Solitary creamy white flowers appear in summer. Self-seeds readily and is easy to grow in a sunny site.

ABOVE: Dianthus deltoides *(dwarf pink)*

Edraianthus graminifolius

Very similar to campanula, this charming plant forms small tufts of grass-like foliage up to 4in (10cm) in height, with clusters of purple-blue bell-shaped flowers in late spring and summer. Prefers full sun. This plant is not easy to cultivate and is therefore not recommended for beginners.

Epilobium glabellum

A native of New Zealand, this delicate plant grows to a height of 6in (15cm) with masses of cream or pink flowers in summer. Plant in a sunny area.

in mid-summer. Prefers full sun and acid soil.

Erica cinerea
Bell heather

This shrub has an open growing habit and rose-purple blooms from late spring through summer. A white form is also available. Choose a sunny position and make sure the soil is slightly acid in pH.

Erica herbacea
Heath

There are many forms of this delightful small shrub, which flowers in winter. It will reach a height of 10in (25cm) and is studded with urn-like rose-pink flowers. An easily cultivated evergreen. Prefers a sunny position and, like all the heathers, an acid soil.

Erigeron alpinus
Alpine fleabane

In a sunny position with good drainage, this perennial will thrive and bear dense flower heads of mauve-pink and yellow during summer. Looks wonderful in a massed planting.

ABOVE: Eranthis hyemalis *(winter aconite)*

Eranthis hyemalis
Winter aconite

A hardy plant that will thrive in most conditions but prefers a well-drained loam soil in a partially shaded area. The small yellow flowers appear in early spring and are circled by glossy green leaves.

Erica ciliaris
Dorset heath

There are more than 500 different heathers, many of which are suited to growing in rockery gardens. This one reaches a height of 2ft 9in (80cm), and has soft leaves with pale undersides, and brilliant rose-purple flowers

Erigeron karvinskianus
Fleabane

A wonderful plant for rocky crevices and planting between paving. It is a perennial with small white daisy flowers, tinged with pink, over many months during summer and autumn.

Erinus alpinus
Fairy foxglove

A delightful small perennial that resembles a tiny foxglove, with rose-purple flowers in spring. Ideal for growing in rocky crevices or over dry stone wall.

Erodium chrysanthum
Storksbill

The plants in this group are very similar to geraniums. This species forms clumps of silvery, fern-like foliage, and is covered in bright yellow flowers during late spring and early summer. Male and female flowers are on separate plants. Easy to grow. Plant in full sun.

Erysimum cheiri
(syn. Cheiranthus cheiri)
Wallflower

A popular plant with a few cultivars that are suitable for the rock garden. The tiny 'Harpur Crewe' is the best, with its fragrant yellow flowers. Plant in a sunny position. An easy-to-grow plant for beginners.

Euphorbia cyparissias
Cyprus spurge

A tuft-forming plant with a spreading habit and fir-tree-like foliage. Oblong heads of golden-yellow flowers appear during spring. Plant in full sun or partial shade. Can be invasive, so ensure roots are contained.

ABOVE: Erica cinerea *'alba minor' (bell heather)*

ABOVE: Euryops acraeus

Euphorbia mysinites
Spurge

Particularly good for rockeries, this fleshy plant has blue-grey foliage and large yellow-green flower heads in summer. Cut back after flowering to encourage new growth. Prefers full sun.

Euryops acraeus

A shrubby perennial, forming a dome of grey-green, waxy foliage. Bright yellow flower heads bloom during late spring and early summer. Easily cultivated in a sunny spot.

Gaultheria procumbens
Creeping wintergreen

An extremely hardy creeping shrub, growing to a height of 6in (15cm). The glossy leaves are aromatic, while the drooping white blooms are flushed with pink. Prefers a sheltered area and acid soil.

Genista sagitallis
Winged greenweed

This easy-to-cultivate mat-forming shrub has a spreading habit and bright yellow flowers in spring and summer. Can be planted in full sun or partial shade.

Genista tinctoria
Dyer's greenweed

A small shrub, growing to 3ft (1m) tall. The yellow flowers are pea-like and were once used extensively as a yellow dye. Easily cultivated, it prefers full sun and well-drained soil.

Gentiana acaulis
Trumpet gentian

This large group of plants has many species that are popular in alpine and rockery gardens. This one has brilliant deep blue, funnel-shaped flowers that are carried on short stems above the foliage during spring. Can be temperamental, and should be positioned in semi-shade.

Gentiana sino-ornata
Gentian

Noted for its prostrate spreading stems supporting solitary terminal blooms and its covering of narrow, pointed leaves. The blooms appear in autumn and are a rich blue, alternating with greeny yellow. Prefers acid soil and a semi-shaded situation.

Geranium dalmaticum
Cranesbill

Another large group commonly grown in alpine and rock gardens. This species is very hardy, with glossy green foliage and rich pink flowers in late spring and early summer. Plant in either full sun or partial shade. An easy-to-grow variety, good for the inexperienced gardener. Any of the smaller cranesbills are worthwhile in this situation.

ABOVE: Genista sagitallis *(winged greenweed)*

ABOVE: Hebe pinguifolia

Geum reptans
Creeping avens

A rather difficult but beautiful perennial, forming tufts of soft green foliage with long red runners that break off to form new plants. Golden-yellow flowers appear in summer. Requires a great deal of sunshine and a moist, acid soil.

Globularia incandescens

A low-growing, cushion-shaped perennial with blue-grey foliage and violet-blue flowers in late spring and summer. Grows well in a scree garden.

Gypsophila repens

A hardy species with a low-spreading habit. The foliage is grey-green and the tiny flowers can be white or pink, forming a cloud above the foliage. Plant in a sunny position. Easy to grow.

Haberlea rhodopensis

A crevice-loving plant with rosettes of hairy, bright green foliage and pale lilac flowers that are similar to foxgloves. Needs plenty of moisture and a semi-shaded situation.

Hebe pinguifolia

A native of New Zealand, this small shrub has leathery grey-green foliage and dense white flower spikes during spring and summer. Will thrive in most conditions, but prefers a sunny position. Several other Hebe species are also excellent for the rockery.

Helianthemum nummularium
Rock rose

A charming evergreen shrub with grey-green foliage and masses of yellow flowers during summer. Prefers a sunny position and needs heavy pruning after flowering. Can be grown in crevices or between pavers. Many worthwhile cultivars.

Helichrysum bellioides
Everlasting

Forms a low carpet with a spread of up to 2ft (60cm). The branches are covered in a distinctive white "wool". Creamy white flower heads are produced in summer. Prefers full sun and a warm climate. Not an easy plant to cultivate.

Helleborus niger
Christmas rose

Prized for its glossy deep green foliage and large white cup-shaped flowers. Blooms appear in winter and early spring. Easy to cultivate in a shady, sheltered position.

Hepatica nobilis

A widespread species, related to the anemones, that grows best in moist leafy soil in a sheltered position. Foliage is deep green and kidney-shaped, while flowers are in shades of white, pink, bluish purple, and even red (the Scandinavian species).

Heuchera racemosa

An attractive plant that forms a downy tuft of long-stalked leaves, with flower stems reaching a height of 10in (25cm). These stems carry racemes of flowers that are white, with a yellow-green calyx. Easy to cultivate. Prefers full sun.

Houstonia caerulea
Bluets

A mat-forming perennial with glossy foliage and masses of tiny china blue flowers with pointed petals, produced throughout summer. Easily cultivated in a sheltered position.

ABOVE: Hepatica nobilis

Hypericum balearicum
St John's wort

A low-growing shrub with leathery foliage. The leaves have distinct warty growths on their surface. Deep golden flowers appear from late spring through summer. Very hardy, easy to grow in rock crevices or between pavers.

Hypericum reptans

There are several worthwhile species for the rockery. This one has a prostrate spreading habit, with bright red buds that open to golden-yellow flowers in summer. This species is excellent trailing over a rock wall or as a crevice planting, in sun or partial shade.

Iberis saxatilis
Candytuft

A branching evergreen shrub that reaches a height of about 5in (12cm). White flowers cover the plant during late spring and early summer. Choose a sunny position.

Iberis semperflorens
Candytuft

This delightful plant forms a mat of deep green foliage that spreads to about 3ft (1m). Masses of white flowers are carried against the foliage throughout spring. Easy to grow, prefers a sunny position.

Kalmia angustifolia

A small evergreen shrub with pleasant foliage and outstanding panicles of reddish pink or ruby-red flowers during summer. Plant in a sunny position, in slightly acid soil.

Lamium maculatum
Deadnettle

An aromatic perennial with stems up to 6in (15cm) tall. The leaves are often marked with a silvery or pale patch in the centre. Pinkish purple flowers appear from spring through to autumn. Very adaptable; however, inclined to be invasive.

Lavandula stoechas
Lavender

With stems up to 2ft (60cm) tall and powerfully aromatic grey-blue leaves and blue flower spikes, the lavender is popular but temperamental. Requires a great deal of sun in a sheltered site with well-drained soil.

Leontopodium alpinum
Edelweiss

One of the most popular alpine plants, edelweiss forms a tuft of grey-green hairy leaves with willowy flower stems. Yellow-white flowers bloom in spring and summer. Easy to cultivate, often planted in scree beds or between paving stones. Prefers full sun.

Leptospermum humifusum

A wonderful spreading shrub, growing to a height of 9in (23cm). Red stems covered with thick foliage, and studded with tiny white flowers during spring and summer. Full sun and an acid soil are essential requirements.

Lewisia cotyledon

An outstanding rockery plant, easy to grow, with fleshy leaves and large panicles of salmon through to crimson, apricot or orange flowers during spring and early summer. Requires a warm, sunny position.

Limnanthes douglasii

A hardy annual with fern-like foliage, growing to a height of 10in (25cm). Blooms are white, flushed with lemon-yellow in the centre, and are produced during late spring and summer. Easy to grow in sun or partial shade.

Limonium bellidifolium
Statice/sea lavender

A compact clump of mid green foliage, and tiny lilac-pink papery flowers. Plant in a sunny corner.

ABOVE: Lamium maculatum *(deadnettle)*

Linaria alpina
Alpine toadflax

A short-lived perennial with a low-trailing growth habit and blue-green foliage, covered with masses of violet and orange flowers from spring through to autumn. Easily grown in a sunny position.

Linum perenne

A tufted perennial with delicate grey-green foliage, and flowers in many shades of blue during summer. Easy to grow, this small plant will thrive in full sun.

Lobelia syphilitica

A dwarf perennial with a neat growing habit and large blue flowers during autumn. Easily cultivated in most soils, in sun or partial shade.

Lupinus confertus
Lupin

A perennial with slender stems, bearing blue and white pea-like flowers in summer. Ideal for the back of the rockery, planted in full sun.

Lupinus lylii
Lupin

This pretty perennial forms a leafy mat of silver or grey foliage to a height of 4in (10cm). Slender stems and blue flowers are carried above the foliage in summer. Easy to grow in a sunny area with a gritty soil.

Lysimachia nummularia
Creeping Jenny

A mat-forming perennial with a prostrate habit and brilliant yellow flowers during spring and summer. Easily cultivated in deep, well-drained soil. Can be invasive, so cut back after flowering.

Mattholia fruticulosa
Stocks

A perennial with hairy foliage and yellow-brown to purple-red fragrant flowers in summer. Thrives in a sheltered site with protection from early spring frosts.

Mazus pumilio

A creeping perennial with short, leafy branches and white or white-blue flowers, flushed with yellow in the centre. This plant prefers full sun.

Meconopsis cambrica
Welsh poppy

This easily cultivated poppy forms an upright tuft of pale green foliage. Bright yellow rumpled flowers are produced in summer. Prefers a partially shaded position.

ABOVE: Meconopsis cambrica *(Welsh poppy)*

ABOVE: Myosotis alpestris *(alpine forget-me-not)*

Mimulus luteus
Monkey flower

A perennial with lush green foliage and bright yellow blooms during summer. Easy to grow in sun or partial shade.

Myosotis alpestris
Alpine forget-me-not

This perennial forms a tuft of foliage up to 8in (20cm) tall. Tiny blue flowers, flushed with yellow in the centre, are dotted over the plant in summer. Plant in a sunny area with moisture-retentive soil.

Oenothera acaulis
Evening primrose

A delightful dwarf species with a low-growing habit and toothed grey-green foliage. Large white blooms turn pink as they age and bloom during summer and into fall (autumn). Plant in full sun.

Omphalodes verna
Blue-eyed Mary

A trailing perennial reaching a height of 6in (15cm). Leaves heart-shaped, flowers blue, and prolific in spring. Plant in sun or partial shade. Can be invasive.

Ononis rotundifolia
Rest harrow

A deciduous shrub that forms rounded bush up to 20in (50cm) tall. Both stems and leaves are covered with fine hairs, and the rose-pink or white flowers are borne in racemes during spring and summer.

Origanum dictamnus
Marjoram

An aromatic herb that requires a sunny, sheltered position. Forms a tuft of hair-covered leaves up to 8in (20cm) tall. Drooping flower heads have pink blooms during summer and autumn.

Oxalis enneaphylla
Oxalis

A charming small perennial with rounded leaves and large cup-shaped white flowers in late spring and early summer. Easy to grow and non-invasive.

Paeonia cambessedesii

A dwarf peony with grey-green foliage that has a distinctive metallic sheen. Deep rose blooms with a central cluster of yellow stamens appear in summer. Plant in a sunny position.

Papaver alpinum
Alpine poppy

A short-lived perennial that forms a tuft of grey-green foliage and golden-yellow or white flowers, carried on long stalks. Easily cultivated, especially in a warm sunny area.

Penestemon davidsonii

A variable species, usually forming a creeping mat of foliage, with lavender or violet flowers carried on stalks in summer. Requires a warm, sunny position and light well-drained soil, and is a good plant for scree beds or between pavers.

Phlox douglasii
Phlox

A neat, low-growing plant with prickly foliage and masses of mauve flowers in late spring. Many excellent cultivars with red, crimson, white, or lilac flowers. Easy to grow if drainage is excellent.

Phyllodoce cosmosa

A beautiful evergreen shrub with a low-creeping habit. The foliage is a glossy dark green and the lilac-purple flowers

ABOVE: Paeonia cambessedesii

are borne near the stem tips in late spring and summer. Plant in full sun with acid soil.

Phyteuma globulariifolium

A tiny perennial with tufts of leaves to a height of about 2in (5cm). Deep violet flowers appear in summer and

autumn. Plant in a sheltered position with partial shade and acid soil.

Plantago nivalis
Broad-leaved plantain

Grows to a height of 2in (5cm), with leaf rosettes covered in fine,

silvery hairs. Grey-green flowers are carried on stalks in late spring and early summer. Plant in a sunny position.

Platycodon grandiflorum
Balloon flower

An herbaceous perennial with upright stems covered in blue-green leaves. Large bell-shaped blue or purple flowers are produced during summer. Easy to grow in a sunny spot; however, can be invasive.

Polygala chamaebuxus
Milkwort

This easy-to-cultivate plant has leathery foliage. Flowers are either white or yellow, with red wings appearing in summer. Requires a moist, lime-free soil and partial shade.

Polygonum affine

A mat-forming perennial, growing to 9in (22cm) tall, with leathery deep green leaves, fading to bronze in autumn. The rose-red flowers bloom in summer. Easy to grow in most conditions.

Potentilla fruticosa
Shrubby cinquefoil

A dense shrub up to about 3ft (1m) tall, with delicate foliage that is shed in autumn. Brilliant yellow blooms are produced in small clusters during summer. Plant in an open position and it will thrive.

ABOVE: Polygala chamaebuxus *(milkwort)*

Pratia pendunculata

A carpeting perennial with pale green foliage and mauve-pink flowers on long stalks during summer and fall (autumn). Easy to grow; prefers partial shade. Can be invasive.

Primula allionii

A mound former with masses of leaf rosettes. During spring a profusion of small magenta flowers appears, each with a striking white eye. Ensure it has a moist soil and some shade shelter.

Primula auricula

An easily cultivated plant with large fleshy leaves and slender stalks of pale to deep yellow flowers during spring. Plant in full sun or partial shade.

Primula clarkei

A small species with finely toothed foliage and rose-pink blooms in spring. Requires a lot of moisture and some shelter from summer sun.

Primula denticulata
Drumstick primula

Easily cultivated, this charming perennial has masses of pale mauve to deep purple funnel-shaped flowers in early spring. Survives most conditions, and can be planted in the shade.

ABOVE: A cultivar of Primula auricula

ABOVE: Primula sieboldii

Primula hirsuta

A variable species, with sticky, toothed foliage and magenta to mauve flowers in spring. Easily cultivated in full sun or partial shade.

Primula japonica

A popular plant, with finely toothed leaves and many red or purple flowers in spring and summer. Easy to grow in moist loamy soil, in semi-shade.

Primula sieboldii

Downy leaves are held on long slender stalks and die back after flowering. Flowers are white, pale pink or pink-purple, appearing in late spring and summer. Easy to grow in partial shade.

Primula vulgaris

This charming plant has delicate yellow flowers during spring. Can be temperamental unless planted in a sheltered position.

Prunus prostrata

A deciduous shrub rarely exceeding 1ft (30cm) in height. Has small, toothed leaves and almond-shaped pink blossom in spring. Requires a well-drained sunny site.

Pulsatilla vernalis
Spring pasque flower

A tiny plant, growing to a height of 10cm (4in). Flowers are woolly and pink, each white in the centre with a cluster of golden stamens. Easy to grow in full sun.

ABOVE: Rhodohypoxis baurii

Raoulia sp.
Scabweed, vegetable sheep

An interesting group, native to Australia and New Zealand, forming mats of silvery foliage. Some very easy to grow, others temperamental. Ideal for scree beds and between pavers.

Rhododendron campylogynum

A spreading shrub up to 4ft 6in (1.3m) in height, with glossy deep green foliage and cream or pink bell-like flowers in late spring. Prefers partial shade and an alkaline soil.

Rhododendron forrestii

A robust but sometimes difficult-to-cultivate shrub with large, deep red, bell-shaped flowers in spring. Plant in a sheltered position and ensure that the soil is alkaline.

Rhodohypoxis baurii

A small, tufted plant up to 3in (8cm) in height with rose, carmine or pale pink flowers in spring. Plant in well-drained but moist soil.

Ramonda myconi

Forms a flat spread of deep green foliage up to 25cm (10in) across. Violet-like flowers are carried above the foliage during spring. Long lived and drought resistant, ideal for crevice planting.

Ranunculus calandriniodes
Mountain buttercup

The grey leaves have a striking scalloped edge and the poppy-like blooms are large and snowy white with a pink tinge. These appear during winter. A hardy plant, preferring a sunny site.

Ranunculus paranassifolius
Alpine buttercup

A small species, with dark green foliage and white flowers that turn pink or reddish as they age. Plant in a sunny position and do not allow the soil to dry out.

Salix reticulata
Dwarf willow

A prostrate species that becomes woody with age. Glossy oval leaves are covered with a net of veins and are a striking silver. Long-stalked catkins appear in summer. Prefers partial shade.

Sanguinaria canadensis

A handsome tufted perennial, with grey-green foliage and anemone-like flowers that appear in spring. Flowers are white, with a central cluster of yellow stamens. Easy to grow in a sheltered position, in alkaline soil.

Saponaria caespitosa
Soapwort

A cushion-forming perennial with pointed foliage and dense clusters of purple-pink flowers in summer. Easy to grow. Prefers an open, sunny position.

Saxifraga sp.
Rockfoil

A genus of over 350 species, which are generally perennials. Considered one of the backbones of the alpine or rockery garden. Foliage varies greatly according to the species. Flowers, usually in the blue-purple range, bloom in spring and summer. Most species are easily cultivated and therefore make excellent plants for the beginner. As the common name suggests, ideal for planting in rock crevices or over dry walls.

Scabiosa graminifolia

A charming plant that forms tufts of silvery grey leaves up to 8in (20cm) tall. Lavender-pink flowers heads appear during summer. Easy to grow in a sunny position. Can be frost tender.

Scutellaria alpina
Alpine skullcap

This interesting perennial forms a spreading tuft foliage up to 8in (20cm) across. The hooded, upright flowers are borne in clusters during summer, and are rich purple with a white lower lip. Easily grown in full sun.

Sedum
Stonecrop

A large genus of about 600 species of succulent plants, many of which are ideal in rockeries. They have fleshy leaves and clusters of star-like flowers in summer. Most are easily grown. Prefer a well-drained, gritty soil.

ABOVE: Saxifraga oppositifolia (*rockfoil*)

Sempervivum sp.
Housesleek

A genus of hardy succulents that are ideal for growing in walls or crevices. Most have rosettes of fleshy, pointed leaves and starry flowers; many attractive cultivars. Very hardy and easy to grow, ideal for inexperienced gardeners.

Shortia uniflora

A clump-forming shrubby plant with toothed leathery leaves and pale pink, sweetly scented flowers in spring. Can be grown in full sun or semi-shade. Prefers alkaline soil.

Silene alpestris

A rambling, tufted perennial with sprays of white flowers in summer. Easy to cultivate, especially in an open, sunny position.

Soldanella alpina

A dainty plant that forms a mat of thick dark green leaves The bell-shaped flowers are violet or bluish, and appear in spring. Plant in a sunny position in alkaline soil.

Stachys corsica

A delightful small perennial that forms a spreading mat of glossy foliage, reaching a height of 2¹/₂in (6cm). Flower vary in hue from snowy white to deep purple, and appear in summer. Prefers an open, sunny position.

ABOVE: Sedum pulchellum *(stonecrop)*

Tanacetum densum

An herbaceous plant with spreading, delicate silver-grey foliage. Leaves are almost fern-like in appearance. Flowers are insignificant. Plant in a sunny, sheltered aspect with well-drained soil.

Teucrium chamaedrys

A small shrub growing to a height of 9in (22cm), with glossy dark green foliage and leafy flower spikes that range from pale to deep purple. Easily cultivated in sun with well-drained soil.

Thalictrum alpinum
Meadow rue

A tiny plant, with fern-like foliage. Dainty violet flowers, gold in the centre, appear in summer. Prefers a gritty, well-drained soil.

Thymus serpyllum
Wild thyme

An aromatic, spreading plant with mid green foliage and rose-pink to rich purple flowers in spring. Easy to grow in a sunny position.

Trifolium repens
White clover

A perennial herb that can be invasive, with long-stalked foliage and white to pale pink flowers during spring and summer. Prefers a sunny, open site.

ABOVE: Trillium erectum

Trillium erectum

A handsome plant with deep green, mottled foliage and reddish purple flowers in spring. Easily cultivated in a sheltered position.

Trollius acaulis
Globe flower

A perennial with brilliant green foliage, growing to 5in (12cm). The golden-yellow flowers unfurl to flat saucers during summer. Will thrive in most conditions in well-drained soil.

Vaccinium uliginosum

An upright shrub, growing to a height of 30in (75cm), with blue or grey-green foliage, and pink flowers and black berries in spring and summer. Prefers partial shade and alkaline soil.

Verbascum x 'letitia'

A compact shrub, with grey-green leaves and primrose-yellow flower spikes in summer. Prefers a sheltered, warm site with lots of sun.

Veronica nummularia
Speedwell

A mat former, growing to 5¹/₂in (14cm), with small, rounded leaves and blue or pink flowers, carried in summer. Thrives in sun or partial shade in moist soil. There are several other veronicas also suitable for the rock garden.

ABOVE: Viola cornuta (horned pansy)

Viola canina
Dog-toothed violet

Forms a spreading mat of deep green leaves with deep blue flowers in spring and summer. Each bloom has a green or white spur. Plant in partial shade. Can be invasive; however, very easy for beginners to grow.

Viola cornuta
Horned pansy

A charming plant with deep green, toothed leaves and fragrant violet or lilac flowers produced during spring. Easy to grow in sun or in partial shade. Ideal for inexperienced gardeners.

Viola lutea
Mountain pansy

Easy to cultivate, this pansy flowers in summer, with blooms that are yellow through violet and white. Can be grown in full sun or semi-shade. Easy to cultivate. Self-seeds and spreads around the garden.

Viola odorata
Violet

This delightful plant has long runners with plantlets at the tips, creating a carpeting effect. Toothed leaves are studded with fragrant white or violet flowers in late spring and summer. Prefers a shaded position.

Wahlenbergia albomarginata

A tufted perennial growing to a height of 7in (18cm), with either blue or white bell-shaped flowers. Easily cultivated in full sun or partial shade.

Waldsteinia ternata

A mat-forming perennial with distinctive foliage and rich yellow flowers in spring. Thrives in most conditions and soils.

RIGHT: Waldsteinia ternata

Index

Photography credits

Harry Smith Horticultural Photographic Collection, front cover; Charles Mann, back cover; The Garden Picture Library (J.S. Sira), pp.2-3; Charles Mann, p.4; The Garden Picture Library (J.S. Sira), p.5; Charles Mann, p.6; Photos Horticultural, pp. 8-9; Charles Mann, p.10; Charles Mann, p.12; Photos Horticultural, p.14; Photos Horticultural, p.15; Charles Mann, pp.16-17; Clive Nichols, p.18; Harry Smith Collection, p.20; The Garden Picture Library, p.21; Charles Mann, p.24; The Garden Picture Library (John Glover), p.28; Photos Horticultural, p.32; Harry Smith Horticultrual Photographic Collection, p.36; The Garden Picture Library (John Glover), p.37; Photos Horticultural, p.40; Clive Nichols, p.44; The Garden Picture Library (Jerry Pavia), p.48; Photos Horticultural, pp. 52-53; Photos Horticultural, p.54; Charles Mann, p.56; Photos Horticultural, p.57; Photos Horticultural, p.58; Charles Mann, p.59, p.60, p.61; The Garden Picture Library (Jerry Pavia), p.63; Charles Mann, pp.64-65; Harry Smith Collection, p.66; Charles Mann, p.68; Photo|Nats (Priscilla Connell), p.69; Photos Horticultural, p.70, p.71; Clive Nichols, p.71; Photos Horticultural, p.72; Charles Mann, p.73, p.74, p.75; Photos Horticultural, pp. 76-77; Charles Mann, p.78, p.80; Photos Horticultural, p.81; Photos Horticultural, p. 82; Charles Mann, p.83; The Garden Picture Library (Clive Nichols), pp.84-85; The Garden Picture Libary (Steven Wooster, Designer A. Noel), p.86; The Garden Picture Library (Bob Challinor), p. 88; Charles Mann, p.89; Clive Nichols, p.90; Harry Smith Collection, p.91; The Garden Picture Library (John Glover), pp.92-93; Photos Horticultural, p.94, p.96, p.97left, p.97right, p.98, p.99; Charles Mann, p.100; Photos Horticultural, p.101; Photos Horticultural, p. 102; The Garden Picture Library, p.103; Photos Horticultural, p.104,; Photos Horticultural, p.105; The Garden Picture Library (Clive Nichols), p.106; Photos Horticultural, p.107; Photos Horticultural, p.108; Charles Mann, p.109; The Garden Picture Library (Brian Carter), p.110; The Garden Picture Library (Clive Nichols), p .111; The Garden Picture Library (Didier Willery), p.112; The Garden Picture Library (Brian Carter), p.113; Photos Horticultural, p.114, p.115, p.116, p.117, p.118; Charles Mann, p.119; Photos Horticultural, p.120, p.121, p.122, p.123, p.124; Charles Mann, endpapers

Published by Lansdowne Publishing Pty Ltd
Level 5, 70 George Street, Sydney NSW 2000, Australia

First published 1994
Reprinted 1995

Managing Director: Jane Curry
Production Manager: Sally Stokes
Publishing Manager: Deborah Nixon
Designer: Kathie Baxter Smith
Illustrators: Valerie Price, Mike Gorman (line drawings)
Copy Editor: Avril Janks
Picture Researchers: Jane Lewis, Kate Oliver

Formatted in Garamond 3 on Quark Xpress
Printed in Singapore by Kyodo Printing Co. (S'pore) Pte Ltd

ISBN 1 86302 281 3.

Front cover: *A colourful display of perennials and rockery plants thrive in an informal, cottage-style rockery garden.*
Back cover: *Rocks provide an ideal framework for the cultivation of a wide range of plants, including ferns and succulents.*
Endpapers: *The use of rocks and moss in Japanese landscape design.*
Title page: *The startling pink and white blooms of* Lewisia cotyledon.
Opposite contents page: *The powerful, fleshy texture of* Sempervivum *sp. bedded between rocks.*
Page 5: *The spectacular yellow blooms of* Adonis vernalis *set against a backdrop of vivid green foliage.*